T0368419

EMBRACING LIFE

UNDERSTANDING FATE

Emeka Obi Anyiam

WestBow Press books may be ordered through booksellers or by contacting:

WestBow Press
A Division of Thomas Nelson & Zondervan
1663 Liberty Drive
Bloomington, IN 47403
www.westbowpress.com
844-714-3454

Because of the dynamic nature of the Internet, any web addresses or links contained in this book may have changed since publication and may no longer be valid. The views expressed in this work are solely those of the author and do not necessarily reflect the views of the publisher, and the publisher hereby disclaims any responsibility for them.

Any people depicted in stock imagery provided by Getty Images are models, and such images are being used for illustrative purposes only.
Certain stock imagery © Getty Images.

Scriptures taken from the Holy Bible, New International Version®, NIV®. Copyright © 1973, 1978, 1984, 2011 by Biblica, Inc.™ Used by permission of Zondervan. All rights reserved worldwide. www.zondervan.com The "NIV" and "New International Version" are trademarks registered in the United States Patent and Trademark Office by Biblica, Inc.®

ISBN: 979-8-3850-0053-1 (sc)
ISBN: 979-8-3850-0054-8 (hc)
ISBN: 979-8-3850-0055-5 (e)

Library of Congress Control Number: 2023911190

Print information available on the last page.

WestBow Press rev. date: 08/15/2023

WESTBOW
PRESS®
A DIVISION OF THOMAS NELSON
& ZONDERVAN

It is a privilege to dedicate this book to my best friend, Marian Janette Marietta, who passed away suddenly on September 2, 2020.

Even though you are gone, death cannot erase the marks your heart left on earth that were filled with love, compassion, grace, and kindness. You were special to me and everyone around you. You have tightly secured a place in my heart, and you will remain my best friend until we meet again. RIP, best friend.

CONTENTS

PREFACE

Have you ever gone to the grocery store to buy seedless fruit, such as watermelon or oranges, but when you got home, you discovered it was not seedless after all? The sign at the store indicated the fruit was seedless. Instead of making the purchase based on your own life experiences, you figured the store must know about its product. Unfortunately, you were disappointed by the outcome.

How about the time you used a fast-food drive-up window because you were craving a particular sandwich? You knew exactly what you wanted to order and were ready for that first bite. You ordered the sandwich with only mayonnaise, lettuce, and ketchup. After you drove off, you took a bite of your sandwich—and got a mouth full of pickles and mustard. It is safe to say your meal was ruined.

Life has a way of throwing a wrench in our plans. I've been there, and I know what it feels like. When this happens to the important things in life, it can be destabilizing. You may wonder if you caused it to happen somehow. Self-doubt may take hold, and that can be scary. So, out of all the watermelons and oranges in that store, you picked the one full of seeds. This is a great example of fate and its unexpected effect on us all. Unfortunately, we do not have control over our destiny, even though we do have self-will, which we always should exercise. Only God has total control.

How does self-will fit into our lives? What role does it play in our day-to-day living? If we are powerless over fate, does that mean that we should ignore our self-will? Absolutely not! Self-will is the ability to do whatever we want, whenever we want. Our self-will could either contribute to our growth or cause our downfall. These are the minor annoyances that happen in our daily lives that leave us wondering "Why me?" Sometimes, we let disappointment cripple us. Instead, we should ask ourselves, "Why is this happening? What is it trying to tell me? What does it mean? What is it preventing? Is it creating a pathway to a better outcome down the road?"

The title of this book, *Embracing Life: Understanding Fate*; explains and expands on the notion that things are meant to happen in the way they are meant to happen, exactly when they are meant to happen. This book will help you understand how to effectively look at things from a different perspective, how your self-will can make or break you, and how to deal with unfavorable events in a way that helps, not hurts. By understanding fate and the power of self-will, you can live a more fruitful life, regardless of whatever gets in your way.

Sometimes, you might have to drive on a road full of potholes to get to a better destination. If you are interested in learning how life works, then you need to understand how fate (which only God controls) and self-will contribute to where you land, as well as the experiences you have along the way. All the songs selected for this book are relevant to the sections they were placed in.

CHAPTER 1

REALITY OF LIFE AS IT IS

It Is What It Is

Have you ever found a product in a store that you had to have and felt you must buy before someone else got their hands on it? Maybe it was slightly damaged, but it was the only one left. A voice told you to buy it, and that voice was so loud that your rational thoughts were pushed out of your mind. Ideas may have flooded your mind as to how you could fix the must-have item, as well as where in your house you should place it. A rational and still small voice told you this might be a bad decision, but nothing could change your mind. One of the store managers informed you that the product was "sold as is" and was not eligible for return. The manager further explained why another customer had returned it, but in your mind, that did not matter, even though you would have no opportunity to return the product in the future. Some problem-solving steps ran through your mind, assuring you that everything would be OK and that whatever issue it had could be tweaked, amended, or fixed.

Sometimes we take chances or risks because that's our human nature. We have so many interests and things we value. But I wonder how much we value our own lives. From my perspective, I view life "as is." Once we are born into this world, there is no return to sender.

Remember, even new products can be defective. Nobody is born perfect, as each individual has his or her own defects or deficiencies. We amend, tweak, fix, change, and adjust as we grow from one developmental stage to another.

Positive and Negative Impacts of Our Thoughts

Human beings cannot exist without thinking. "If our minds are messed up, our lifestyles are messed up, and when our lifestyles are messed up, our mental and physical health suffer" (Leaf 2021, 25). It is difficult not to think and worry constantly, regardless of when or where or who we are. We must deal with thinking constantly; it's part of our living arrangement that cannot be avoided or eliminated. We start thinking from the second we wake up in the morning until we fall asleep at night. In some cases, we are even haunted by our thoughts in our dreams.

In her book *The Secret*, Rhonda Byrne (2006, 16) states,

> Whether we realize it or not, we are thinking most of the time. If you are speaking, or listening to someone, you are thinking. If you are reading the newspaper or watching television, you are thinking. When you recall memories from your past, you are thinking. When you are considering something in your future, you are thinking. When you are driving you are thinking. When you are getting ready in the morning, you are thinking.

Our thinking could lead us to the right path or the wrong path. The law of attraction states that positive thoughts always yield positive outcomes, but negative thoughts always yield negative outcomes. Our negative thinking steers us toward the wrong paths or makes life unbearable. The more we let negative thoughts overshadow or overcrowd our minds, the more we feel overwhelmed and the deeper we dig our holes. We become emotionally paralyzed, which manifests in our physical bodies with health issues.

There is nothing wrong with processing our experiences at any given time, but we should balance our negative and positive thoughts as much as possible. In order to make better decisions or take steps that could eliminate circumstances that cause those thoughts, we must notice the types of thoughts we have. Consider the *National Geographic* program that showed hyenas ripping apart a living warthog—that is exactly what happens psychologically when we dwell on negative thoughts. Dwelling on negative thinking increases our stress levels and can rip us apart, just like hyenas rip apart their living prey. We might love to entertain those thoughts because that's all we know. From my experience, just having positive thoughts is not enough. We must take necessary steps to achieve our goals and objectives. The Bible says, "Faith by itself, if not accompanied by action, is dead" (James 2:17 NIV).

In her book *Cleaning Up Your Mental Mess* (2021, 15), Dr. Caroline Leaf states,

> A large part of the problem is that we've lost much of our ability to think deeply. We've forgotten the art of deep and focused mind-management. We want things fast, quick, now. We often don't want to put in the hard work that leads to true change, or we've never been taught what this kind of work looks like.

Without a shadow of doubt, our efforts matter a great deal as we strive to think more positively. We also must put in the work necessary to get out of our emotional holes where we are trapped and held hostage. We cannot lay on our hands and think good thoughts only and expect manna to fall from heaven. Biblically, manna was a miraculous type of food God provided for the Israelites during their exit from Egypt. Miracles do happen, of course, but physical efforts must be applied. We cannot deny the inevitable—our thoughts. Nonetheless, it is wise and necessary to carefully process those negative thoughts and experiences and then come to terms with them by embracing the fact that whatever happened was meant to happen that way. Without acknowledgment, we are stuck and cannot move forward.

> Your thoughts are like an ivy plant. They can either protect you by acting like a thermal shield, or they will poison your soul. (Anyiam 2019, 75)

Thought Management

The struggle we face is not about the good feelings but the bad ones. How do we control or manage them in order to stay afloat and to keep moving forward? In her book *Cleaning Up Your Mental Mess*, Dr. Caroline Leaf (2021, 31) states,

> I believe we live in a day where the mismanagement of mind has reached a zenith … A large part of the problem is that we've lost much of the ability to think deeply. We've forgotten the art of deep and focused mind-management. We want things fast, quick, now. We often don't want to put in the hard work that leads to true change, or we've never been taught what this kind of work looks like.

I agree with her statements, and she did list steps to meet this objective. There are many ways that work, but the following strategies worked for me in the past:

1. Understand what you are feeling, and embrace or accept those feelings, as they make you whole.
2. Identify constructive activities that would help you feel relaxed.
3. Once relaxed, refocus on the positives happening right now, and then reminisce about past personal triumphs.
4. Develop a course of action to resolve the issue and stabilize your emotions.
5. Seek help immediately from professionals or healthy support systems, if needed.

Why is it necessary to embrace or lean into uncomfortable feelings?

1. It helps us think clearly or process what's going on with us, accurately and effectively.
2. It could reduce psychotropic dependence. It's imperative to consult a doctor regarding psychotropic medications. A lot of people do not like feeling uncomfortable. Therefore, psychotropic medications become an answer to everything, which could lead to mental destruction. Often, we do not think of psychotropic medications when we are feeling good.
3. It empowers us or keeps us in control of the situation or our thoughts and feelings.

A close friend once told me, "When you're feeling down, dress the best you can because it helps you feel a lot better." The most lethal or healthy aspects of our lives are our thoughts and what we do with them. The more we worry or obsess over our failures or circumstances, without implementing appropriate steps to guide us, the weaker we feel, resulting in our energy being distributed unequally. We could become prey to someone who will take advantage of us.

In his book *Anxious for Nothing*, Max Lucado (2017, 5) states, "Anxiety takes our breath, for sure. If only that were all it took. It also takes our sleep, our energy, our well-being." The amount of energy we invest in our past negative experiences could be invested in our present and future to stay afloat in life.

A friend once confided in me about his mediocre life and how much he hated waking up in the morning—that was the time of day when he was flooded with his failures and other life challenges. He explained that the time between 6:00 a.m. and 8:30 a.m. was a full-blown psychological battle for him. It was when he did his devotions and completed other morning tasks before heading out to work for the day. He despised that time because his type of work barely paid his bills. While doing his usual morning duties, his mind was flooded by despair to the point that he was emotionally crippled, as if he were paralyzed.

As I listened to him, I related what he was saying to what Britt Frank (2022) said in her book *The Science of Stuck*:

> Stuck in the "I should" spiral of self-judgment. Stuck in the family pressure. Stuck in the shutdown mode, unable to make the leap between what you know you should do and what you actually do.

My friend was constantly behind on his payments, resulting in those bills being sent to collections. There were many failed promises made to his fiancée, and he felt like a complete failure. He did not disclose these psychological battles to her because he did not want her to worry, to see him as vulnerable, or to break up with him. He kept borrowing money from colleagues without any assurance he could pay them back. As a result, he could not even leave his house to spend time with friends and family. He specifically listed some of his struggles, such as feelings of loneliness, even though he had a fiancée and was planning to get married. Nothing mattered to him other than being able to independently support himself and his future wife. He said he constantly worried, and he prayed that his circumstances would change for the better, but he could see no light at the end of the tunnel. He also shared that he had dreams many times in which everything he dreamed for came true, but then he woke up to find it was just an empty dream.

Sometimes, he questioned his existence, causing him to feel even more depressed and wondering if he would ever escape from the traps of his circumstances. He pushed through every day but wished that 6:00–8:30 a.m. could be eliminated from his life. His main desire and battle were about his need to make ends meet.

It is beneficial to show your vulnerability to the ones you love, as suffering alone is lonely and could be lethal. You should not feel alone.

Every one of us has a storyline, and regardless of what we do the majority of the time, we can pass through each storyline at any moment. Some of those storylines appear to be awful. Fate may sneak in at any time to tweak or reshape our plans and objectives. The reasons may be shady or unclear at the beginning, and they may not make any sense. This may or may not lead you back to the drawing board. In his book, *Essays on Fate and Illusions*, Ralph Waldo Emerson wrote, "Fate involves melioration" (2010, 32). This means that when fate acts, it is not necessarily bad but could be a way to advance you.

Regardless of on which side of the bed we wake up, we are made to keep planning and moving forward; that's our human nature. We must refuse to settle with our difficult circumstances. We are human, and we are allowed to process those challenging circumstances. We, however, cannot unpack and settle in them. Alan H.

Cohen states in his book, *Why Your Life Sucks: And What You Can Do about It*, "If you settle for less than what you really want, you will get exactly that. If you expect your life to suck, it will" (2002, 18).

Fate and Unexpected Circumstances

My understanding of fate is that it is the outside force, over which we have no control, that establishes our preordained paths in life. Only God has that control.

One of my morning duties is to take a walk. While I was walking one day, I saw a friend and stopped to chat with him. We discussed a whole spectrum of topics within a few minutes, but one that stood out to me was his story of a fishing experience. He described how excited he was to catch two big fish, but he could not take pictures because his phone camera wasn't working. It had been working earlier but refused to work at that particular moment. It was clear he was not too happy about it. He also told me, however, that he moved to a different spot, caught two bigger fish, and was able to take their pictures. So his camera would not work at the first spot but worked at the second spot. As he shared this information, my thought was simply, *Fate at work*. I offered my two cents by letting him know it was not meant for him to take pictures at first, but it *was* meant for him to take the pictures after he moved to a different spot. I did not know why his phone camera didn't work at first, but that was the way it was meant to work out that day.

That is exactly how fate works. When we play rock-paper-scissors, we do not know who will win, but we get the result right then and there. With fate, it is impossible to know. Our circumstances do not own us, but we own our circumstances, good or bad. Our need and drive to survive and succeed and the ability to manage the resources we have at each juncture matter a great deal. Expect changes and tweaks, however, along the way.

Fate can go in several unexpected directions or come from different angles. Fate is that part of life circumstances that plays an invisible role that we do not perceive, think about, or make room for in our daily living and plans. Fate is always out of mind, and its role is so sophisticated that it is impossible to detect. Each morning, when we wake up to face the day, there is always a coded message to decipher or a clue or a puzzle, which may or may not make sense, that we may need to put together out of nowhere. Since it is unexpected, it becomes urgent or an emergency. Sometimes, those coded messages or hidden clues are made somewhat visible, even though they could seem blurry at times, but we either choose to brush them off, ignore them, or take them for granted.

Have you ever gotten out of bed, thanked God for being alive that day, completed your morning duties and devotions, and then asked yourself, "What does life have for me today? What coded message will I work on today? What will life teach or show me today? How will it affect my plans for the day? What if my plans for the day clash with unexpected circumstances? What part will God play in my life today?"

The more we ask these questions, the more we are inclined to proceed carefully and also have room for adjustments in case fate strikes. On second thought, I am not sure we are fully ready at all times. Because we tend to rush through things in life, we miss a lot of steps or miss the point about what life is trying to teach us.

There are twenty-four hours in a day. Depending on our schedules, we may have to manage about ten to sixteen hours while we're awake and in operation. Realistically, there will be twists and turns within that time frame that could make, break, adjust, or change our lives significantly. We must embrace and understand the roles fate plays in our lives. By doing so, we have a better chance of surviving when fate strikes not in our favor. The best fate defense is faith in God. Therefore, our ability to manage the sources of our depression or anxiety and our ability to make quick and lasting adjustments will strengthen. Imagine what life would look like if everything we planned went accordingly, without fate's involvement or interruptions.

What would your world look like? Have you ever considered that those interruptions and tweaks by fate could have prevented something worse from happening? If you were given an opportunity to view the end result of that particular plan you created, just for six seconds, you might understand the other side of fate that you never think about or see, which could result in your abandoning that plan. Fate asks this question: "Why ruin the surprise?" Be alert and be willing to accept life circumstances as they are so that you can keep pressing on. If you can't beat fate at its game, then join it.

Understanding the Person You Are and Your Destiny

Have you ever asked yourself, "Who am I?" One way I have handled my life is to first understand who I really am. That question helped steer me toward the right path. It has helped me remain as consistent as possible. I am still a work in progress and will be throughout my life, but I have mastered my strengths and weaknesses. Also, I have been working on using the resources I have around me so I can combat those weaknesses.

I can't get rid of the weaknesses; they are here to stay. The first step to healing is to embrace them. There is no other way. Who I am matters a great deal to God and to me. I have a purpose in life, and it's my ultimate goal to fulfill that purpose before I pass on. The best way to survive and succeed is to embrace the whole you, regardless of your circumstances. I am very fortunate that I came from an excellent family. There are eight of us, and I am the youngest. I never thought I would leave Nigeria until my parents told me, through my eldest sister, to pack my belongings. In our culture, once they spoke, I had no choice but to follow through with their plan. I wasn't sure at first because of the unknown.

Upon my arrival to the United States on January 1, 1991, people to whom I am not related treated me in a way that was amazing. Fate led me here, and the force behind all of it was God. My brother was here already, and he taught me many things. His recommendations led me to find Crossroads Church in Clifton, New Jersey, where the congregation adopted me as one of their own. One of my college sponsors mandated that I take an aptitude test before starting college. An aptitude test measures our cognitive abilities, work-related behaviors, and personality traits. It examines our ability to work with numbers, logic, and problem-solving skills, as related to the work environment. The aptitude test I took then led me to my destiny. Destiny is the ability to control or shape one's future. We can shape our destinies, based on the choices we make.

Before I left Nigeria, I had graduated from high school and had no interest in going to college. I felt that earning my education was not a "thing" for me. I hated school and had no interest in changing my mind. Back then, my goal was to own a hospital that I could manage. That failed. Instead, my father obtained a job for me to work with his close friend who managed wholesale pharmaceutical drugs. I thought that was the worst job I had ever worked. I despised it and slept a lot during work hours because it was extremely boring. I was fired from that job. Later, one of my sisters got me a position at a printing company. I started off working as a machine operator and later became one of their sales managers. That job lasted until I was informed that I was leaving the country.

Right after taking the aptitude test, I began school and majored in business administration. I struggled immensely with developmental courses, but I was thankful for my adviser, Maria Medina, who stood by me throughout my struggles. She was the best adviser I've ever had, and I am thankful that we are still friends to this day. I don't consider the people who helped me throughout my stay in New Jersey as resources; I consider them family.

I thought I was doomed and felt like I did not belong in school because I could not pass the developmental course in reading. It held me back until Maria came to my rescue and advised me to take the standardized exam in English as a Second Language. I passed it with flying colors, and that led me to proceed with my major. I was fully surrounded by loved ones and supporters who never stopped believing in me. Even though I despised school, I fought through it.

The moral of my story is that I had a dream in Nigeria that did not come to pass due to fate. It did not stop me, however, from dreaming, even though it did not happen in the way I thought it would happen. I learned that I did not have to sit and wait for it to come to me. I had to understand who I really am in order to pursue my dream. I realized that the only option left for me was education. The still small voice in me consistently said that to reach my destiny, I would have to focus on my education. Later, I earned my graduate degrees.

A Destiny Story about Cheyenne Rivers

God always has a target in mind, and He never misfires. To me, I felt like the last quarter would never end. Then, I was reminded of this: "But do not forget this. Dear friends: With the Lord, a day is like a thousand years and a thousand years like a day" (2 Peter 3:8). Our mindsets and God's are not the same. We may look at things from a narrow-minded point of view (North to South with an end in sight), but God looks at things from an east-to-west perspective with no end in sight. This simply means that He sees the whole picture of each circumstance. The depth of His vision for us is immeasurable.

As humans, we crave an instant or temporary fix. God is always after a permanent fix, if only we would let Him. We may not understand it now but might find out after the storm passes. At times, He might not reveal the reason why things happened the way they did, but we must trust Him by believing that He will get us through the storms, and those storms had a purpose.

I was given the privilege to know why the storm occurred in that last quarter of 2021. That challenging circumstance led to me to pay off my student loan. I also learned more than I thought I knew about the process of running a mental health agency. We may despise storms, regardless of how long they last; it is human nature to do so, but there is always an end and good reasons for every storm. They are not always bad. Even if we did not get something out of it physically, we must have gained something spiritually.

You might have experienced writing an essay in school, which your teacher then corrected. If you received your essay back with many corrections on it, you might have felt that the teacher did not like you or that she was trying to humiliate you. In fact, the teacher was not doing those things but was trying to teach you the best way to write and communicate your thoughts and feelings. Overall, even though we might have disliked some of our teachers, they did contribute to our success. Could God be doing the same with us? Yes. In the same manner, we write, and God corrects and then gives back to us what we wrote.

I would like to share what destiny looks like. In his book *A Life Living Fate*, Larry W. Livingston described the life of a woman named Cheyenne Rivers as follows:

> What did Cheyenne want to do with her life? She knew it was not fishing. She even wasn't sure she wanted to go to college and if she did, which one? She went to the state's unemployment office and asked to take the job aptitude test. She was interested in seeing what she would be most suited for as a job. The test revealed that she was highly suited to be a pharmacist. Cheyenne was shocked when she heard those results. That was out of the blue for her to hear. She thought it was a glitch or mistake. The more she thought about that profession, the more she liked the possibility of being a pharmacist. It was an inside job in a clean environment. She was in a position of meeting people, maybe a boyfriend. What about her dyslexia? Would that disqualify her from becoming a pharmacist? She was going to investigate if she could be accepted into that profession. As she dug into the possibility of entering that profession, she found that it was almost impossible to be accepted into that field. It seemed that any profession that dealt with money, numbers or peoples Well-being was too big a risk. She was surprised to find that there were many fields she wouldn't be allowed to participate in. Cheyenne went on the internet to see what people with dyslexia are best suited for in the job market. It was a small list; but one that got her attention was photography. That word struck a hidden nerve and a spot in her brain. She loved that revelation and wondered why she hadn't seen or felt it before. She enrolled at the University of Washington starting the next fall in photography. She was back in school with her brother Eric again. [...] She was amazed to see the studio where she would be working with stars and celebrities. The darkroom was more than she could have ever imagined. It had every piece of equipment that one could have. There wasn't one thing in the photography world that couldn't be done. Cheyenne thought she had seen it all, but when she was shown her office, it took her breath away. The fact that it was located on the fortieth floor should have dawned on her earlier. It wasn't a corner office, but it was large and spacious. One window took up the entire wall. She guessed it to be eight feet tall and twenty feet long. It did have a Center support that made it two individual sections. The view of the bay and San Francisco was something for her to behold. "That's the end of the tour of Cheyenne. Your badge is on your desk and you must keep it with you at all times. You can't gain access to anything without having it scanned and that includes the restroom. I'll leave you to settle into your office," Robert said as he departed. Cheyenne stood in silence looking out the window. She couldn't believe her life at that moment. A great job with great pay and doing something she loved to do. The thought of meeting stars and important people was sweet icing on the cake. She didn't know that when she pressed the LL button on the elevator, that it would take her to the basement. As the doors on the elevator opened, she smelled the aroma of fried chicken and the noise of many conversations from people having lunch. She got in line and purchased a chicken salad for her lunch. Once she had

satisfied her hunger, she spent the rest of the day wandering the floors and meeting people. She was glad to find everyone was pleasant and friendly. She returned to her office and Pam was there waiting for her. "Cheyenne, I forgot to give you your pager. We all carry one so that we can be contacted wherever we are. I put a job assignment on your desk for tomorrow's shoot." "Thank you, Pam." Pam left and Cheyenne opened the packet that was on her desk. Her eyes opened wide and a smile ear to ear spread across her face. She was going to be taking pictures of Lance Bright. (2020, 67)

Against all odds, Cheyenne never gave up. She fought through her disabilities and still made it to her destiny. She knew where she'd come from and who she was. She understood her limitations but was also aware of her strengths. Even though the aptitude test revealed the impossible for her, she did not stop there. She continued to persevere by doing her own research.

Your destiny is waiting for you. Your destiny is not marked "free of charge." It requires a lot of effort and sacrifices to attain it. When you seek it, you will find it. If you don't—well, you know what the answer is. Nothing happens. Imagine what could have happened if Cheyenne had given up?

In the introduction to her book, *The Science of Stuck*, Britt Frank states,

You're not lazy. You're not crazy. You're not weak, dumb, broken, defective, or lacking in willpower. And despite what your nagging inner critic tells you, you don't have a motivation problem. There's something else behind your discarded self-care plans, abandoned to-do-lists, and neglected goals. And the way forward is simpler than you'd think. (2022, 1)

What if we were meant to do the things we don't like or take the paths we despise to reach our full potentials?

Socioeconomic Status Impact

Another unfortunate reality about life is that we have to come to terms with our socioeconomic status. By definition, socioeconomic status is a way of defining individuals based on their education, income, or different types of jobs. It is often grouped as low, medium, and high. Many sociologists are not in agreement on how many social classes exist, but in the United States, there are about four Socio-economic classes—lower class, middle class, working class, and upper class. The higher up a person is on a totem pole, the more access the person has to financial, educational, social, and health resources. It is always vice versa with regard to low-income–class members. Unfortunately, we do not have any control over the family into which we are born. That is our fate.

Just like Cheyenne, however, our destinies could reverse our realities. The first step to success is to accept that fact. There's a sad part, though—there is a saying, "The majority rules." Well, in a democratic state or country, the majority rules. This concept is based on the fact that the greater number should exercise more power than the lesser number. In reality, however, the minority rules or governs instead of the majority. The minority are the rich individuals, and the majority are the poor individuals. It's a battle between the rich and the poor, between the haves and the have-nots. The haves are running the have-nots. This is not physical warfare but psychological warfare. This doesn't happen only in the United States. It happens around the world. From my knowledge, the term *majority rules* is an oxymoron.

According to the United States Census Bureau report, the US population, as of this writing, is 332,911,562. It is estimated that 5.4 percent of the American population earns a six-figure income per year. Also, according to the report disclosed by the IRS in 2018, 0.35 percent of Americans made a seven-figure income that year. Only 1.13 percent of American households made it into the decamillionaire category. According to a Bloomberg article on October 8, 2021, Alexandre Tanzi and Mike Dorning reported that the top 1 percent of the US households hold more wealth than all of the middle class. Based on this article, lower-class households could not be found in the equation. Income earners for middle and lower classes continue to decline, while the top 1 percent of earners hold the bargaining chips. By the end of 2021, the top 1 percent owned 32.3 percent of the nation's wealth.

According to CNBC's Robert Frank, just in 2021, the wealth of the top 1 percent increased by $6.5 trillion. From my perspective and based on our economy as of this writing, it appears that the middle-income families are barely making ends meet. Can you imagine what is happening to the lower-class earners? The poor get poorer, and the rich get richer. The rich have all the resources to navigate themselves through the system, while the poor stay stuck. Does that sound like equal opportunity? No. The gap continues to tilt. It is not tilting toward the majority but toward a small fraction of the population. In his book, *Wealth Inequality in America*, Dr. James Glenn wrote,

> The problem most people cannot see is not that there are rich people or even there is a large gap between the wealth of the rich and middle class, but that the rich are getting richer at the expense of the middle class. Wealth redistribution from the bottom and middle up, not from the top down aided and abetted by central banking and monetary policy is how the rich get richer year-after-year, decade-after-decade. (2020, 2).

Policies and decisions are made from the top, not from the bottom.

You can see from the picture I painted that the majority of Americans live paycheck to paycheck. Some can barely make ends meet. Some are behind on their bills. Most of those unpaid bills are sent to collection, and people are being hunted down to pay what they owe. Some do not know where to find resources or help or how to come up with the next meal for their families. Some are hopeless; they believe that the rate of their survival is very low and that they should give up. They feel stuck and cannot breathe as they face their brutal circumstances.

The rich are the ones at the steering wheel. That tiny fraction of the US population are the ones influencing the policies of the government on a regular basis. They dictate what we do, what we eat, what we own, what we believe, and so on. It appears as if we are at their beck and call.

> The wealth inequality issue is not simply one of who owns a better car, wears finer clothes, or takes fancier vacations. It also governs fundamental aspects of our lives, such as what neighborhoods we live in, what environmental and health hazards we are exposed to, the quality of schools our children attend, and how attentive politicians are to our concerns. Given these stakes, debate on policies to reduce wealth inequality will undoubtedly continue to occupy a central place in American politics over the next decade. (Kinsley 2021, 64)

Politicians make lots of promises on which they cannot follow through. The only person who cares about you is *you*. Only you can make things happen, with God's help. I have heard a lot of people say they wish they'd been born into a wealthy family. Sometimes, I have to remind myself that being on the top is not always a happy place to be. It does have its drawbacks, but until you fully accept your fate, believe in yourself, and keep persevering, you will continue to be a puppet of that tiny fraction of the population that controls the assets of this nation.

Your disabilities and shortcomings should not determine or predict your future. Your destiny determines it, but it requires hard work to make it there. Even though the resources around you are limited, you should go above and beyond to find them. If it means walking an extra mile or ten miles, be determined to do so. If you have to crawl to get there, so be it. It's all about your mindset. There are many success stories of people who had nothing but made their way to the top. The picture of where you want to be is already established in your head. It's a real picture. It's a real goal. It's a real dream, but you have to develop a few objectives to help you reach those goals. Don't sit in depression and anxiety, waiting for things to come to you. Seek God's face and pray constantly for strength and determination to conquer each challenge every single day.

On March 10, 1948, Peter Marshall, US Senate chaplain, prayed by saying, "Let us not be content to wait and see what will happen, but give us the determination to make the right things happen" (Library of Congress 2010, 307). Understand and trust that God listens always. He does care and does answer prayers. If you want to be your own person, to be successful and independent, to have a voice in society and contribute to the well-being of society, then you must see beyond your giants.

Max Lucado (2006) said it best in his book *Facing Your Giants*: "You've seen your Godzilla. The question is, is he all you see? (…) Giants. We must face them. Yet we need not face them alone" (4).

If your giants are the only things you see, it will be impossible to make it through.

> Jesus looked at them and said, with man this is impossible, but with God all things are possible. (Matthew 19:26)

Integrating the Whole Self

We face countless challenging circumstances each day—the good, the bad, and the ugly. Everyone has strengths and weaknesses or limitations. Some of my weaknesses include my getting lost easily (I have no sense of direction), being a slow learner, and being naïve and too trusting. I also think that I have Asperger's, ADHD, and dyslexia.

I wrote down my strengths and weaknesses or limitations, stared at my limitations many times, and cried countless times. I compared notes. Then I learned that I could navigate through those weaknesses in order to stay afloat. I realized that those negative characteristics were not going anywhere. They were here to stay. I felt incapable of achieving anything in life. Getting an education didn't make any sense to me—that was only for intelligent people, and I was never on that list. I used to laugh at people who saw positives in me and believed in me. I was not sure what they were seeing or what to make of it. I thought they were out of their minds, as they made no sense to me. But I absorbed everything they said and pondered over their comments. I doubted myself many times, to the point I felt useless. I thought my goals or dreams were just fantasies and were unachievable, as if they were a joke. When I finally accepted them, a breakthrough happened. My goal, at minimum, was to stay afloat. I finally understood that I had to go through the avenue that I despised most—education—to become somebody.

My fate is how I was; my destiny is who I choose to become. I wish life was that simple. I wish I could snap my fingers and make things happen. In his book *God Will Help You*, Max Lucado states,

> If only we could order life the way we order gourmet coffee. Wouldn't you love to mix and match the ingredients of your future? "Give me a tall, extra-hot cup of adventure, cut the dangers, with two shots of good health."
>
> "A decaf brew of longevity, please, with a sprinkle of fertility. God is heavy on agility and cuts the disability."
>
> "I'll have a pleasure mocha with extra stirrings of indulgence. Make sure it's consequence free."
>
> "I'll go with a grande happy-latte, with a dollop of love, sprinkled with Caribbean retirement."
>
> Take me to that coffee shop. Too bad it doesn't exist. Truth is, life often hands us a concoction entirely different from the one we requested. (2020, 143)

When you integrate the good, bad, and ugly of life into your whole, you have already won. You have taken the first step to success. Fate says, "At each particular circumstance, not everything has to make sense to make sense." One story that didn't make sense but made sense was the story of Abraham, who was one hundred years old when he had his only son, Isaac.

God said to Abraham,

> "Take your son, your only son, whom you love, and go to the region of Moriah. Sacrifice him there as a burnt offering on one of the mountains I will tell you about. … As two of them went on together, Isaac spoke up and said to his father Abraham, "Father?" "Yes, my son?" Abraham replied. "The fire and wood are here," "Isaac said, "but where is the lamb for the burnt offering?" Abraham answered, "God himself will provide the lamb for the burnt offering, my son." … But the angel of the Lord called out to him from heaven, "Abraham! Abraham!" "Here I am" he replied." "Do not lay a hand on the boy," he said. "Do not do anything to him. Now I know you fear God, because you have not withheld from me your son, your only son." Abraham looked up and there in a thicket he saw a ram caught by its horns. He went over and took the ram and sacrificed it as a burnt offering instead of his son. (Genesis 22:2–13)

The chapter appeared to not make any sense, but at the end, it made sense. This man did not waver; he prepared to sacrifice one of the most important things he had waited one hundred years to have. He did not question God because he knew that "to obey is better than sacrifice, and to heed is better than the fat of rams" (1 Samuel 15:22). Now, that makes sense, doesn't it?

I realized that I have to give it all, even if I have to take a route that I despise to get to my destination. That was Abraham's fate, but he never lost faith and did not stop obeying.

Destiny says, "I am not cheap. I require hard work. But you have a choice to either work hard to achieve or just think positively but not achieve." Putting life's puzzles together takes time and effort. You can start with one piece at a time. One piece of puzzle could be getting out of bed in the morning, telling yourself one positive thing about your existence, going to a career center to explore what life has to offer, developing a résumé, looking into colleges or getting your GED, telling a trusted friend what's actually going on with you—just take one step at a time.

To get out of the control of others and the system, you must get out of your comfort zone. Always rely on your strengths more than on your weaknesses. Let God manage the weaknesses. The routes you avoid could be the routes you need to take in order to be successful. So far, those routes do not involve crime of any kind. Don't let anyone pull your string. Educate yourself, and let God take the wheel.

CHAPTER 2

THE PURSUIT OF SELF-KNOWLEDGE AND SELF-DISCOVERY

The Person in the Mirror

If a man empties his purse into his head no man can take it away from him. An investment in knowledge always pays the best interest. (Library of Congress 2010, 185)

Before I proceed with this chapter, I need to caution you that some of the language presented in this chapter may be a bit challenging to understand. I will present terms or concepts that you may not have heard before. You may need some guidance by using a dictionary or consulting with someone who may have more knowledge in these areas than you do.

The pursuit of finding life's meaning starts by learning and understanding who and what you are. There is a lot to learn and understand about the self. Doing so will help you to deal with fate effectively and also help you identify what your destiny is. Let's compare the words *learn* and *invest*. As the *Little Oxford English Dictionary and Thesaurus* tells us, "To learn is to gain knowledge of or a skill in; become aware of; memorize. To invest means to use money, time, etc. to earn interest or profit" (2003, 361). Why do people invest their time in learning about things, places, and people but forget to learn or invest in themselves? Places, things, and other people are so intriguing, but why do some people find themselves less intriguing?

I consider learning about things, places, and people to be self-nurturing, but to some individuals, learning and understanding themselves are more intriguing. While the knowledge and understanding of things, places, and people matter a great deal, knowledge of and understanding ourselves matters most because our survival or destiny depends on it.

I conducted a basic interview with twenty-five people. The question I posed to each of them was, "Tell me the positives about yourself." Thirteen of the twenty-five presented only their negative characteristics. Seven out of those thirteen turned to their partners for help with identifying the positives. When I asked the question again, they laughed and could not respond. Seven out of the twenty-five were flabbergasted and asked why I wanted to know. I asked that question because they did not have an answer. They smiled. Five of the twenty-five were able to identify more negatives than positives in themselves, but at least they were able to identify some positives.

I often sense that a lot of people are self-conscious about some of their characteristics, but when asked about their positive characteristics, most gravitate toward their negative features instead.

"Why is that?" I asked.

The response was the same: "I do not know." Maybe it's because of how their brains are wired and that those negative features bother them more than they realized. Many people's upbringings are traumatic in nature, to the point that even positive interaction with someone or hearing empowering questions could trigger unexpected responses or answers. Some may have wondered, *What do you want from me? No one has asked such questions before. Could it be a sincere gesture?* Extenuating circumstances might have triggered their reactions with regard to the questions I asked or because I treated them nicely. M. Sessions has noted, "Have you ever wondered how you became you? Why do you act and think the way you do? It isn't just random luck. You were programmed that way, by your environment and hereditary" (2019, 21). Is it possible that sometimes a person does not want to share his or her positive characteristics to avoid feeling vulnerable?

When you attempt to share your positive traits, your stomach might rumble as if you are about to get sick, and your mind might interfere by not letting you go any further, due to fear of getting hurt or feeling vulnerable. Answering the question by verbalizing your positives could mean you are giving in. Why allow yourself to feel vulnerable? Due to your past experiences, your walls remain up, and you are unable to identify who you really are. I do not blame you, but you are not broken. Your worth is more than you might assume at the moment. It would be wrong to minimize your past negative experiences, and no one should take them lightly.

Dave Mitchell, author of *The Power of Understanding Yourself*, asks,

> So, why take this trip into the library of your mind? Simple. Therein lies the content of me. But you must find it. You must decide to visit space. You must think about what you know, then get up and research what you know so that you can know more. All that noise that you experience each day, both important and not, can drown me out. To find it, you must walk into that quiet library. (2019, 8)

When you put more effort into understanding who you really are, regardless of your past negative experiences, you have taken the first step to healing yourself and breaking those walls. When the COVID-19 pandemic started, we could not go anywhere. Many of us became frustrated and anxious. We wanted to leave the house and feel normal again.

That is how your positive features feel. They don't want to sit still until you learn, understand, and accept them. They want to be seen and heard. It's a story people would love to hear. Your life stories belong to you—your storylines are your storylines. Even though they cannot be altered, you owe it to yourself to embrace them. Make every effort to educate and invest in yourself because the best and longest-lasting education and investment you could ever earn is in yourself.

I don't have all the answers for you, but guess who does? *You.* Why do you need to learn about and understand the person in the mirror? For your own benefit? For your survival? For the sake of your loved ones? For your future? For your destiny? How about freeing yourself from the bondage of your past? Whatever the reason behind your not acknowledging who or what you are, remember that your present or future do not deserve the punishment from your past.

Jane Kise, David Stark, and Sandra Hirsh, coauthors of *LifeKeys: Discovering Who You Are*, write, "These truths about who you are, why you are here, and what you do best can help you find personal pathways to fulfilling work, activities and opportunities for service" (1998, 3).

In order to remain in control of self and regain control of your life's destiny, regardless of what fate throws at you, you must educate yourself in two important ways. First, you must understand yourself from a human point of view. Second, you must understand yourself from a spiritual point of view. Both factors require intellectual ability and motivation, which everyone possesses, even though it may seem gloomy at times. The *Little Oxford English Dictionary* defines *intellect* as "the ability to think logically and understand things" (2003, 356).

Let's start from the human point of view and with the human brain.

The Depth of the Brain and Its Benefits

> Every normal person has a brain and nervous system and is, therefore, endowed with great mental capacities. ... What a thrill it is to know you possess the greatest machine ever conceived, so awesome that it could only be created by God Himself-a brain, nervous system, and the ineffable human mind! (Stone 2016, 5)

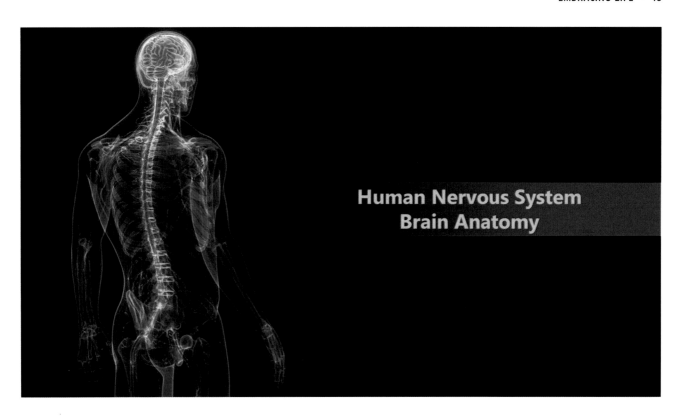

Human Nervous System
Brain Anatomy

Amazing, isn't it? In her book, *How the Brain Works*, Leslie A. Hart defines the brain as follows: "The human brain is an organ of the body that occupies the upper part of the head, fitting into a sturdy container of bone" (1975, 26).

Let's consider a few terms that relate to the connections and operation of the brain: spinal cord, central nervous system, neurology, and neuropsychology. (I might have unintentionally omitted a discipline field that contributes to the healing of the brain, as technology is getting more advanced nowadays, and new disciplines are coming into existence.)

The brain is a very complex and sophisticated part of our beings. In order to comprehend who you are or how you function, you must first understand how your brain operates. In his book *Learning How to Learn: The Ultimate Learning and Memory Instruction*, Jerry Lucas states, "There are only 3 steps in the learning process. They are getting information, learning the information and using the learned information" (2001, 1).

From my professional point of view, the most important and powerful part of the human body is the brain. Without knowing how to manage or operate it, you will be stuck. It is an organ of soft nervous tissue located in the skull that controls thought, memory, emotion, touch, motor skills, vision, breathing, temperature, hunger, and every activity that regulates our bodies.

The spinal cord is a long tubelike tissue that connects the brain to your lower back. Both your brain and your spinal cord constantly work together. Because they communicate with each other on a constant basis, they joined forces and became the central nervous system. The central nervous system controls the activities of the body every second. While neurologists focus on the diseases of the brain and provide medical treatments, neuropsychologists focus on understanding the connection between the brain and behavioral symptoms. This is because any type of disorder in the brain or the nervous system could negatively impact cognition or behavior.

> Most importantly, you can use the knowledge of your brain to improve your everyday functioning, reach your life goals, and improve or overcome cognitive problems such as memory, attention, or verbal problems. It will also help you understand how emotional problems such as depression, anxiety, or mood swings affect your cognition and what you can do to help yourself in these areas (...). Knowing how your brain works is powerful, because what you don't know could kill you. If you know what works well in your brain and what doesn't, for example, which of your brain functions eat string and which are weak—you can learn how to use the good parts to compensate for those that aren't so good. (Koltuska-Haskin 2020, 162)

You cannot function well if your central nervous system is not stable or balanced. But how do you maintain a balanced system?

Maintaining a Balanced Central Nervous System through Self-Care

In *The Brain: The Story of You*, author David Eagleman writes,

> Our thoughts and our dreams, our memories and experiences all arise from this strange neural material. Who we are is found within its intricate firing patterns of electrochemical pulses. When that activity stops, so do we. When that activity changes character, due to injury or drugs, you change character in lockstep. Unlike any other part of the body, if you damage a small piece of the brain, who you are is likely to change radically. (2015, 5)

You have no choice but to thoroughly care for yourself, both mentally and physically. There are multiple factors to consider with regard to your health. A neurological or neuropsychic evaluation has many benefits. To pursue such an evaluation, please consult with your primary care physician (PCP) for guidance and recommendations. A PCP is a health care practitioner who sees individuals, with or without medical conditions, on a routine basis. Once you obtain medical insurance coverage, a PCP could be assigned to you. You also have an opportunity to choose who your PCP will be, as long as that PCP is in your insurance provider's network. If you do not have a PCP, it would be best to consult with your medical insurance company for leads. You can also contact your insurance provider to obtain a list of medical doctors in their network and your location.

Your PCP or your insurance network provider can refer you to a neuropsychologist within their network who will schedule and complete your evaluation and explain the results with you. This evaluation may be included in your benefits package.

Information online may not be trustworthy or accurate. Please avoid engaging in an online self-test and diagnosis. Self-diagnosis is very dangerous and could do you more harm than good. You cannot do it yourself; seek outside help. No one can operate a car without its engine.

On a different note, I understand that life is very busy. We live in a fast-paced world. We get so busy that we forget to nurture ourselves or meet our own needs. We often make time, however, to give other people advice—sometimes solicited and sometimes unsolicited. That's our human nature. We love to chip in our two cents, even though we might not have experienced that same circumstance as the person we're advising. The advice we give others may be concrete, great, sincere, logical, and helpful, but it's also wise to listen to our own advice and implement the strategies we gave to others. We would be on the road to success if we could apply to ourselves at least 25 percent of what we tell others.

Is it possible that when you're advising someone else, you're unconsciously referring to yourself? Maybe or maybe not. So why listen to your own advice? Because your instincts said so. To maintain a stable and balanced central nervous system, you must implement steps such as exercising daily, getting enough sleep (between seven and nine hours each night), eating healthfully, getting some sunlight, drinking at least half a gallon of water or more each a day (consult with your PCP for guidance), taking appropriate medication, following through with all medical appointments, and not engaging in substance abuse, which can slightly hurt your brain functioning. Everyone's brain activities are different. To acquire the best result or improve your well-being, consult with your primary physician. Recommendations differ from one person to another, depending on your health, how active you are, or where you reside. (There could be more factors that I don't know but that you know work effectively for you. Engage in them, as long as they're legal.)

Self-care is very important and should not be ignored. It takes motivation, determination, and consistency to get the job done. It is your life and your story. When fate fires a shot at you or punches you unexpectedly, being in a balanced health position can make it bearable. We value a lot of different things in life. Those visible or tangible items we value are priceless to us, even though they may be worthless to another individual. If we value things that are tangible, why is it so difficult to value and care for important things that are in us? Think about that for a minute.

In *Your Blueprint for Life*, author Michael Kendrick offers the following scenario:

> Imagine you are taking a trip. This is not just a trip; it's the vacation of a lifetime. The car is packed. The route is planned. The reservations are made. Everything is in place. As your family members fasten their seatbelts, anticipation filled the air. But as you turn the key, something else

fills the air: smoke. It's the thick, blue kind that looks like it won't clear up anytime soon. Next thing you know, you hear a loud rattling sound from under the hood and the engine suddenly stops. Vacation over. Your body is like a car. It's your "transportation for life." If you neglect or abuse it, just like a car, it's more likely to break down. (2015, 151)

You make time for everyone. Start making time for yourself.

Maintaining Balanced Mental Health

From the moment you wake in the morning, you're surrounded with a rush of light and sounds and smells. Your senses are flooded. All you have to do is show up every day, and without thought or effort, you are immersed in the irrefutable reality of the world. But how much of this is a construction of your brain, taking place only inside your head? (Eagleman 2015, 17)

What goes on in your head (psychologically) can be good, bad, or ugly. Your mental well-being is another factor you must examine and take seriously. While you work on maintaining a balanced central nervous system (physical), don't ignore your mental health (psychological) needs. Mental health deals with your psychological and emotional well-being. The physical and the mental health aspects of your life work hand in hand. They are like twins. They are interconnected. Your central nervous system watches and stands by. It utilizes special cells, called neutrons, to send signals throughout your body.

If the steps I identified in Chapter 1 didn't work, explore other resources around you, such as counseling. Do the best you can to explore resources so you can battle back, including seeking professional assistance. Whatever is happening to you psychologically can negatively impact your physical health, leading to ulcer, stroke, heart attack, or nervous breakdown and can even be fatal. Some feel that seeking mental health services shows weakness or is embarrassing. You are protected, however, by the Health Insurance Portability and Accountability Act of 1996 (HIPAA). HIPAA is a federal law created to protect patients' sensitive information from being revealed without the patients' consent or knowledge. Everything is kept confidential.

The bottom line is that if you are battling something that refuses to go away, your ultimate goal should be to make it disappear so you can regain control. There is no shame in pursuing that avenue. Not seeking help could make you look weaker, and your suffering could get worse. Also, it could result in a more severe mental health issue, which could be even more unbearable. The earlier you begin, the better it will be for you. Again, avoid searching on the internet to diagnose yourself. Conducting your own inquiry without professional health could make you believe that your symptoms indicate a diagnosis that is inaccurate. Each individual must meet particular criteria for a particular diagnosis.

Some people struggle with insurance coverage. If you don't have health insurance, do thorough research; there may be resources that could help you. Never give up. You have the capability to identify whether your challenging circumstance is a psychological, medical, or spiritual battle. If it's psychological, seek mental health help. If it's physical, seek medical help. If it's spiritual, go to God with it.

Now, let's examine the field of mental health—marriage and family therapists, mental health counselors, clinical social workers, psychologists, psychiatrists, targeted case managers, dependency case managers. psychiatric nurses, addiction counselors, Christian counselors, and applied behavioral analysts, to name a few. Psychiatrists have a medical degree, while psychologists have a doctorate in psychology. Both use the Diagnostic and Statistical Manual of Mental Disorders (DSM–5). (Due to the sensitivity of this subject, I will not mention any of the mental health disorders.)

In his book *Clergyman's Psychological Handbook*, Clinton McLemore writes,

Most psychological disorders are best regarded as products of unfavorable experiences and faulty learning rather than as products of physical diseases. The term "illness" should be reserved for individuals whose problems can be traced to a specific biological defect or ailment, such as a brain lesion, barbiturate poisoning, or neurosyphilis. (1974, 22)

In other words, not all mental health disorders are genetic but may be due to the environment or past experiences. Consult your PCP or your insurance provider for possible leads or referrals to a mental health professional. Disciplines collaborate with each other as a community to empower and stabilize individuals and their families. I love and respect everyone in this field. Health care professionals conduct thorough assessments for each individual, and they formulate a treatment plan geared to that individual that will lead to a cure or improve the individual's capability to combat his or her mental disorder effectively. Unfortunately, not all mental health disorders are curable, and some of them are passed down from one generation to another. .

Health care professionals are not there to change your personality. They are available to empower your personality from a constructive point of view, not destructive. They do so by helping you make necessary adjustments or accommodations that will increase your coping mechanisms or empower you to manage the disorder effectively. Consider the following example: Imagine someone walking into your house and saying that you must get rid of everything you have in your home and replace those things with their selected choice of products. You likely would have a serious sit-down conversation to figure out if the person was out of his or her mind and to find out who would fund the replacements. Now, what if the person shows up to your home and gives you tips on how to make adjustments so your home will look more beautiful and less cluttered. Would you be open to that idea?

Mental health professionals work tirelessly to help individuals and their families survive and succeed.

Understanding and Preserving Your Personality Type

> Personality basically refers to those non-physical features of a person's existence that give identity to the person. (Beck 1999, 18)

There is a lot to learn about ourselves. We will continue to evolve. As we transform from one developmental stage to another, life's circumstances (good, bad, and ugly) will continue to happen. Our personalities stay unchanged. Fate remains unpredictable. We must keep learning and mastering ways to combat each circumstance. It is crucial for each individual to preserve his or her personality type. First, however, we have to understand it.

A personality is a set of characteristics that form a person's character. Researching, learning, understanding, and preserving your personality type will strengthen the ways you view situations and deal with outcomes from each situation.

> For starters, knowing your type is important because "being yourself" or "being true to yourself" seems to require that you first, "know yourself." (Drenth 2017, 2)

My point exactly. The approach is the one and only way. You can't bypass it or have option B. Have you ever wondered what it would take for you to get to know yourself? What motivates you? When I've asked these questions, some people froze. Some claimed they knew who they were, and they described their likes and dislikes and what was on their bucket lists in a vague manner. I got the gist of what they were trying to present, but I could tell from some of their facial expressions that they were wondering, "Why ask such bizarre questions?"

These so-called bizarre questions could help you understand or find out if a person is comparable to you or not. You cannot tell, however, unless you have an understanding of who you are first.

> The mind is the man, and the knowledge of the mind. A man is but what he knoweth. (Bacon 1996, 79)

Without self-knowledge, you become stuck in vicious cycles. Personality type has nothing to do with external elements, such as things or places. I am referring to a set of characteristics that form a person's character. Consider the following: You are the big picture. No one else is but you. The minute you recognize and embrace those two facts, you have acknowledged yourself. By definition, self-acknowledgement is when an individual embraces himself or herself as having certain characteristics.

How do we become the persons we are? Should nature be considered? What about nurture? From my knowledge, it's both nature and nurture. There has been an ongoing debate over these two factors. Instead of joining the debate, however, I would rather embrace these two factors as contributing to who we are. Both nature and nurture play important roles in shaping who we are.

In his book, *A User's Guide to the Brain: Perception, Attention, and the Four Theaters of the Brain*, Dr. John Ratey states,

> In reality there is no debate. Most of who we are is a result of the interactions of our genes and our experiences. In some cases, the genes are more important, while in others the environment is more crucial. We tend to oversimplify because we want to identify a single cause of a particular problem, so we can pour our efforts into one "cure." (2001, 31)

Nature is a product of genetics (biological), while nurture is a product of the environment. Just like the brain works side by side with the spinal cord, forming the central nervous system, so do nature and nurture work together to form an individual's personality type; they are inseparable. However, nature is constant, while nurture lacks that factor. One cannot just be a product of his or her environment alone. Neither does nature act alone.

One of the great tools we use when assessing and providing counseling to children and their families is a genogram. The genogram was invented by Murray Bowen.

> Genograms are schematic diagrams listing family members, their relationships to one another, dates of marriage, deaths, and geographical locations. (Nichols 2016, 160)

Using this tool gives clinicians a synopsis of a family's history. Understanding it gives us better strategies to implement in order to psychologically nurse the individual or his family back to health or to a normal level of functioning. This can be a very touchy subject for some individuals, due to traumatic experiences in their family histories, but a family's generational history contributes to the shaping of each person's personality type.

Not everyone has the desire to associate with their families of origin, but to gain some ground in understanding your personality type, it needs to be considered. Seeking help from a mental health professional could help you regain control and conquer your past traumatic fears. You do not need to feel alone.

> The silent impact that our roots can have on our behaviors can be a big surprise. Our cultures and larger cultural histories often set the foundation for our family systems. (Selenee 2021, 31)

While nature is hereditarily genetic, nurture is based on environmental variables, such as how we are raised, social relationships with others, experiences we obtained along the way, culture of the environment, and so forth. The way an individual was nurtured in life, as well as that individual's experiences along the way, leads to personality type growth or lack thereof. Even though the biological aspect of human life is constant, environmental variables can strengthen or bury an individual's personality type. The way in which some people are brought up and pressure from the environment are often the main sources of family disconnection or dissension. We had or did not have control over the ways we were brought up or the things we experienced, but that doesn't determine who we are. We give it more power every second of the day by continuing to feed and nurture those past experiences, resulting in continued feelings of helplessness and hopelessness and feelings of being held captive.

It's a part of human nature and the process. There is nothing wrong with remembering past experiences. You should not ignore traumatic experiences but should have the ability to perceive those experiences in a different light, such as viewing them as teachable moments (what to do or not do), as experiences you conquered. You, not your past, are still in control of your destiny.

In his book *Believe and Achieve: 17 Principles of Success*, W. Clement Stone writes,

> One of the most important lessons of my life forced itself on me at about the time I was graduating from grammar school. It was a lesson that turned into a major principle: You are subject to your environment. Therefore, select the environment that will best develop you toward your desired objective. (...) make sure that you control your environment. Avoid situations, acquaintances, associates, who tend to hold you back. (Stone 2016, 319)

My first thought when I read the above was, *Wow!* So, what does that really mean? Stone explained everything you need to know. It comes down to making choices. Remember that the brain is a complex and sophisticated part of our beings. It has two sides, the right and the left. Each operates differently, as each has its own functions. The right brain is intuitive, creative, and emotional, while the left brain is analytical, logical, and orderly. It doesn't matter if you are more "left-brained" or "right-brained." Some people might use that as an excuse for making bad decisions because they are one and not the other. There is at least one factor on both sides that should help you make better decisions—intuitive from the right side of the brain and logical from the left side of the brain.

Intuitive is your gut feeling, while logic is your judgment. Both factors are active when it comes to making choices. If they do not agree, don't implement that decision, as you may end up regretting it. Think about it more. Remember the saying, "Follow your heart, but take your brain with you." It's a great statement that should not be taken lightly.

Even though we think constantly, taking the time to *actually* think and process a circumstance and make a good decision can be challenging or time-consuming for a lot of people. This is because some people are reluctant to engage in any task (processing situations) that warrants sustained mental and physical efforts. (With mental efforts, you have to correlate logic and intuition; with physical efforts, you have to put that decision into action.) We live in a fast-paced world, where many people don't want to take the time anymore. They would rather get the answer right then and there, or they have the desire for a quick fix. The amount of time that should be invested into correlating intuition and logic can be exhausting, but it is worth doing so.

Is being right- or left-brained part of your personality? Absolutely! We all possess a major tool that should help direct and keep us on the right track. We live in a multicultural society—think of a salad bowl or a melting pot. We constantly interact with those whose paths we cross. In many cases, we have no choice but to do so, and we also gain a lot of experiences through each culture.

A culture should not be based only on from where a person originates. An individual's or a group of individuals' personal lifestyles should be considered a culture. Some lifestyles could strengthen or pave the way to success, and certain others could lead to destruction or even be fatal. Since we possess the most powerful tool—the brain—we should use it to make decisions that will benefit us, not hurt us. We should associate with people who will build us up, not tear us down.

Use both sides of your brain to your advantage. Make better choices, regardless of where you are located. Pick your interests wisely. Do not succumb to peer pressure. Pick individuals who can help you flourish, not wither. Seek individuals from whom you can benefit, not those who will harm you. You have the ability to pick and choose your support system or social network. No one can do that for you; it has to be you. You know what would ruin your life and what would not.

By the way, support systems are made up of people who always will be there when you need help or who positively support you in your life's endeavor. *Social network* refers to your social interactions or personal relationships or individuals with whom you interact. Set clear boundaries for yourself. *Boundary* is defined as, "Emotional and physical barriers that protect and enhance the integrity of individuals, subsystems, and families" (Nichols 2016, 438). Boundaries need to be clear so everyone knows where you stand.

Many individuals come from broken homes. Detachment from loved ones, the people one considers a family, can lead an individual to seek out other individuals or groups as a means to fit in and gain a sense of belonging. Pacts are initiated, which may be good or bad for the individual. I would never judge someone for the choice that person made, but there are positive and negative consequences behind each decision. A *consequence* (positive or negative) is a direct impact or result of an action by an individual. So, choose wisely.

As I was writing this section, I had flashbacks of one of my brothers, someone I looked up to while I was living in Nigeria. He was brilliant—he had a very high IQ—but he made a pact with the wrong crowd and began to use drugs. He lived a very destructive life, with self-inflicted psychological issues. We were brought up in a large, strong, and well-known family back home, even though my father was an alcoholic. Alcoholism did a lot of serious damage to my family. In fact, most of the things I witnessed from my father helped me stay away from abusing alcohol. Even so, I am very proud of my family. The path my brother took was his fate and destiny. And I miss him dearly.

Remember that you can't control your fate, but you can control your destiny. There are a lot of distractions in the world. Be careful that the environment doesn't control you; you should control your environment. The ball is in your court. Every decision you make, every step of the way, will determine your destiny.

Personality-Type Assessments

There are many personality-type assessments, but I have selected only a few to discuss, as these have helped me tremendously.

Everyone is different. My mother used to say that all our fingers are not equal because each person's preferences are different. Whichever one you identify with and believe will give you the most accurate results should be the one you pursue. They include love languages (LL), intelligence quotient (IQ), Myers–Briggs Type Indicator (MBTI), and aptitude tests (AP).

Love language tests emphasize the significance of an individual understanding his or her emotional love language.

> The problem is that we have overlooked one fundamental truth: People speak different love languages. (Chapman 1992, 14)

An emotional love language puts total focus on emotional connections instead of physical connections. This is how a person knows that he or she is loved. Many times, individuals lose themselves in the physical aspect of a relationship, while the emotional aspect suffers. There is more to a person than the physical aspect of love. If that is ignored, it will be difficult to manage who you are or your relationship. I encourage you to review the section headed "Falling in love" in chapter 3 ("How to Express Heartfelt Commitment to Your Mate") of The "Five Love Languages" Focusing only on what the eyes can see while ignoring, intentionally or unintentionally, the emotional aspect of the person you are could lead to frustration, misunderstanding, anxiety, depression, and so forth. The "feeling" (emotional) aspect is lacking in a lot of people and relationships; people may avoid dealing with that aspect, almost as if it's taboo.

These issues often stem from the person's upbringing or how emotions were modeled around the person in his or her social and support networks. Being able to communicate emotional needs to yourself and others strengthens you and also strengthens them—it's a win/win situation.

Understanding your love language will better equip you to communicate your emotional interests. If it's difficult for you, you may need professional assistance and support.

Oh, how we work hard in many ways to succeed and feel loved in life, while at the same time ignoring or refusing to acknowledge that being able to understand ourselves emotionally and communicating it could set us free and improve who we are around others.

Gary Chapman, author of *The Five Love Languages*, says, "Love is the most important word in the English language—and the most confusing" (1992, 19). How can someone express love to you when you don't understand it to communicate it? This goes back to your needing to understand *you* first before others can understand you. Chapman identified the five love languages as words of affirmation, quality time, receiving gifts, acts of service, and physical touch. (His book is available online or at any bookstore.) You can take online quizzes at https://5lovelanguages.com/quizzes/love-language to help you identify your love language, which is beneficial.

Some of the various intelligence measures are intelligence quotient (IQ) tests, the Cattell Culture Fair Intelligence Test, the Stanford-Binet test, and the Wechsler Adult Intelligence Scale. People may have individual preferences, but each test determines an individual's intelligence through selected measurements consisting of spatial recognition, short-term memory, mathematical ability, analytical thinking, and verbal abilities. Each test is structured differently from the others.

There are tests online for measuring your intelligence, but some require payment before the result is released to you. There may be providers in your insurance network who could administer a test to you without your having to pay out of pocket. (Consult your insurance company for recommendations; it's worth looking into.)

Just because someone scores high doesn't mean that person is greater than others or that the person should be condescending toward others. A score should never be used to tease others or mock them. You should not should use it to discriminate against or intimidate others who scored lower than you did. Some intelligent people can't find their way out of a tomato can, but others, who may have scored low on the intelligence scale, could be the one to help you.

You have a lot to offer, both to yourself and others around you. In fact, your personality should help you relate to others better. There may be times when you need to get to other people's level in order for them to comprehend you better—by your tone and how you deliver your thoughts. Remember, regardless of how high your IQ is, you still have some weaknesses.

For me, it is about comprehending who I am and how to attain my needs effectively to be successful. Taking one of the tests I presented to you will help you understand your strengths and your weaknesses. I have used the knowledge I gained from the test to help me identify the best career for me and to understand how I operate on a regular basis. Also, I've identified ways to balance my areas of weakness with my strengths.

In *Ultimate IQ Tests*, authors Ken Russell and Philip Carter note,

> There are many different types of tests. However, a typical test might consist of three sections each testing a different ability, usually comprising verbal reasoning, numerical ability and diagrammatic, or spatial, reasoning. (2015, 2)

The **Myers-Briggs Type Indicator (MBTI)** is tailored to help individuals understand their personality types, strengths, and preferences.

> Typology helps us understand our natural roles and strengths. It also provides valuable guidance and insight with respect to our careers, relationships, and personal growth. (Drenth 2017, 1)

I kept mentioning that no one will understand you unless you first understand yourself. The MBTI is a very good instrument to help you understand yourself better. The first time I came across this assessment, I thought it was a waste of time to answer a few questions that would enhance my knowledge of who I really am. How could that be? I came to find out that this assessment tool played a giant role in placing my feet on the road to success. I highly recommend this assessment.

In her book, *Personality Type: An Owner's Manual* (1998), Lenore Thompson states,

> THIS BOOK IS FOR THOSE WHO BELIEVE that living can be an art—a project whose outcome is ourselves, the person we are meant to be. But how does this happen? How do we become uniquely "ourselves"? Is it possible to create a life in which we are acting from our deepest values-doing the best that we know how? How do we figure out what those values are? Where do they come from?

Well, if you want some of the above questions answered, the MBTI is one of the tools from which answers would come. The MBTI identifies sixteen personality type profiles. They are identified as INFJ, INTJ, INTP, ISTP, INFP, ISFP, ISFJ, ISTJ, ENFP, ENTP, ENFJ, ESFJ, ENTJ, ESTJ, ESFP and ESTP. I am ENFJ.

Kendra Cherry (2022) described Myers-Briggs personality types, as listed below:

- ISTJ HYPERLINK "https://www.verywellmind.com/istj-introversion-sensing-thinking-judgment-2795992"— HYPERLINK "https://www.verywellmind.com/istj-introversion-sensing-thinking-judgment-2795992"The Inspector: Reserved and practical, they tend to be loyal, orderly, and traditional.
- ISTP HYPERLINK "https://www.verywellmind.com/istp-introverted-sensing-thinking-perceiving-2795993"— HYPERLINK "https://www.verywellmind.com/istp-introverted-sensing-thinking-perceiving-2795993"The Crafter: Highly independent, they enjoy new experiences that provide firsthand learning.
- ISFJ HYPERLINK "https://www.verywellmind.com/isfj-introverted-sensing-feeling-judging-2795990"— HYPERLINK "https://www.verywellmind.com/isfj-introverted-sensing-feeling-judging-2795990"The Protector: Warm-hearted and dedicated, they are always ready to protect the people they care about.
- ISFP HYPERLINK "https://www.verywellmind.com/isfp-introverted-sensing-feeling-perceiving-2795991"— HYPERLINK "https://www.verywellmind.com/isfp-introverted-sensing-feeling-perceiving-2795991"The Artist: Easygoing and flexible, they tend to be reserved and artistic.

- INFJ HYPERLINK "https://www.verywellmind.com/infj-introverted-intuitive-feeling-judging-2795978"— HYPERLINK "https://www.verywellmind.com/infj-introverted-intuitive-feeling-judging-2795978"The Advocate: Creative and analytical, they are considered one of the rarest Myers-Briggs types.
- INFP HYPERLINK "https://www.verywellmind.com/infp-a-profile-of-the-idealist-personality-type-2795987"— HYPERLINK "https://www.verywellmind.com/infp-a-profile-of-the-idealist-personality-type-2795987"The Mediator: Idealistic with high values, they strive to make the world a better place.
- INTJ HYPERLINK "https://www.verywellmind.com/intj-introverted-intuitive-thinking-judging-2795988"— HYPERLINK "https://www.verywellmind.com/intj-introverted-intuitive-thinking-judging-2795988"The Architect: Highly logical, they are both very creative and analytical.
- INTP HYPERLINK "https://www.verywellmind.com/intp-introverted-intuitive-thinking-perceiving-2795989"— HYPERLINK "https://www.verywellmind.com/intp-introverted-intuitive-thinking-perceiving-2795989"The Thinker: Quiet and introverted, they are known for having a rich inner world.
- ESTP HYPERLINK "https://www.verywellmind.com/estp-extraverted-sensing-thinking-perceiving-2795986"— HYPERLINK "https://www.verywellmind.com/estp-extraverted-sensing-thinking-perceiving-2795986"The Persuader: Outgoing and dramatic, they enjoy spending time with others and focusing on the here and now.
- ESTJ HYPERLINK "https://www.verywellmind.com/estj-extraverted-sensing-thinking-judging-2795985"— HYPERLINK "https://www.verywellmind.com/estj-extraverted-sensing-thinking-judging-2795985"The Director: Assertive and rule-oriented, they have high principles and a tendency to take charge.
- ESFP HYPERLINK "https://www.verywellmind.com/esfp-extraverted-sensing-feeling-perceiving-2795984"— HYPERLINK "https://www.verywellmind.com/esfp-extraverted-sensing-feeling-perceiving-2795984"The Performer: Outgoing and spontaneous, they enjoy taking center stage.
- ESFJ HYPERLINK "https://www.verywellmind.com/esfj-extraverted-sensing-feeling-judging-2795983"— HYPERLINK "https://www.verywellmind.com/esfj-extraverted-sensing-feeling-judging-2795983"The Caregiver: Soft-hearted and outgoing, they tend to believe the best about other people.
- ENFP HYPERLINK "https://www.verywellmind.com/enfp-an-overview-of-the-champion-personality-type-2795980"— HYPERLINK "https://www.verywellmind.com/enfp-an-overview-of-the-champion-personality-type-2795980"The Champion: Charismatic and energetic, they enjoy situations where they can put their creativity to work.
- ENFJ HYPERLINK "https://www.verywellmind.com/enfj-extraverted-intuitive-feeling-judging-2795979"— HYPERLINK "https://www.verywellmind.com/enfj-extraverted-intuitive-feeling-judging-2795979"The Giver: Loyal and sensitive, they are known for being understanding and generous.
- ENTP HYPERLINK "https://www.verywellmind.com/the-entp-personality-type-and-characteristics-2795982"— HYPERLINK "https://www.verywellmind.com/the-entp-personality-type-and-characteristics-2795982"The Debater: Highly inventive, they love being surrounded by ideas and tend to start many projects (but may struggle to finish them).
- ENTJ HYPERLINK "https://www.verywellmind.com/entj-personality-type-2795981"— HYPERLINK "https://www.verywellmind.com/entj-personality-type-2795981"The Commander: Outspoken and confident, they are great at making plans and organizing projects.

I would encourage you to research this test online at your convenience. You do not need to memorize all these groups of letters; you only need to know yours after taking the test. Some online providers of this test may require payment before releasing the results of the assessment. Again, consult with your medical insurance company as to whether a provider in your network could administer the assessment to you without charge.

An **aptitude test** concentrates on measuring an individual's ability in a specific skill or knowledge in a particular field. Many employers utilize this assessment to determine if an individual is suitable for a particular position. This test could determine if you will be hired. A lot of companies desire to reduce costs and increase their profits. They do not want to waste their time and money on someone who may not be qualified for a particular job. As a result, they test the individual first.

I would recommend that you take the MBTI assessment first to determine who you are and which category you fall in with regard to your personality. Then, pursue a career in that field. I think that you would feel more empowered and be in a better position to pursue a field of work in which you feel most comfortable. Many years ago, I applied for a human resources position in Florida. I was tested and questioned about my knowledge of human resources and Florida laws. Each of those questions sounded foreign to me. I did not get the position. The CEO of that agency, however, thought I'd do much better as a therapist than as Director of Human Resources. In fact, I did excel, and I've never regretted not getting the human resources position.

So, provided aptitude tests are used properly there is 'nothing to lose, but everything to gain' by the use of tests. (Barrett and Barrett 2018, 1)

Be mindful of these tests when seeking a position at any organization.

When you visit places like the bank, the post office, and so forth, for whatever reason, a host might ask for your identification or ask you a series of questions about your identity before he or she will grant you access to your own records. Most of us have accounts online. As an individual, you decide what your password is to each of your online accounts. If you forget your password, you will be asked to answer a couple of security questions. Sometimes, you might forget the answers and feel stuck. You thought you wrote down your password somewhere but can't find it. All of a sudden, your mind goes blank. At that particular moment, frustration, anger, and alarm start pouring in.

These same issues could occur with regard to not knowing who you are, which could be a recipe for disaster in your personal journey. Unless you want people to assume the wrong personality type for you or not respond to your type's needs, you must know yourself first. Your qualities are screaming to be recognized. Discovering yourself will help you manage your few weaknesses. You are not dumb. You are not weak. You are not doomed. You just need to figure yourself out in order to feel better about yourself.

CHAPTER 3

WORK PATHWAY

What Drives a Company?

Now that we understand ourselves and understand that we must be aware of how we react and deal with things that happen in our lives, let's look at how we get through workplace challenges. It is fair to say that the two major places we spend most of our time are our workplaces and our homes. So, what drives a company or organization? Can it be God, best practices, revenue, control? You might have other ideas on what drives a company.

God should be the driver of whatever you or any company does in order for the business or you to be successful. To understand how a company or organization functions, you must understand what drives it. By understanding a company's drive, you will be able to apply your personality type and skills effectively and with confidence. All companies or organizations are driven by something. It is the potential employee's duty to do thorough research to understand what that company or organization stands for. There is nothing wrong with making money—we all have bills to pay, but if there is no love for whatever you do, and your drive is set on making money, you will not last; others behind you will move up, while you are still where you started.

> God expects wholehearted devotion to the task–something every employer, including God, appreciates and expects. (Sherman and Hendricks 1987, 71)

A major part of a company's or organization's drive stems from their mission statements, vision statements, policies, and procedures. Every company or organization around the world, whether for profit or nonprofit, likely has mission or vision statements. Even mom-and-pop shops or other small businesses have a dream, mission, or vision too.

We expect whatever we do to grow and flourish. Regardless of how big or small the business is and regardless of whether you own the business or you're working for someone, you deserve to treat that business better by establishing a mission, vision, and other protocols to help you flourish. If you don't have them, develop them, instead of playing it by ear. Establishing a mission, vision, and other protocols to help you run your business effectively is a gift from God and should not be taken lightly. If you are employed by someone, learn about them because they will help you grow and be successful. If the business doesn't present or review missions, visions, policies, and procedures during training or orientation, ask for them. If you have your own business, don't bury it or take it for granted.

> For the kingdom of heaven is like a man traveling to a far country, who called his own servants and delivered his goods to them. And to one he gave five talents, to another two, and to another one, to each according to his own ability; and immediately he went on a journey. Then he who had received the five talents went and traded with them and made another five talents. And

likewise, he who had received two gained two more also. But he who had received one went and dug in the ground and hid his lord's money. (Matthew 25:14–18)

Listen, life is a gift. Whatever you do is a gift. Never hide, bury, or waste it. Every breath and step you take is a moment for you to shine. You cannot throw it away.

What do mission, vision, policies, and procedures even mean? A mission statement is what the company wants to do now; it describes the focus and values of that company.

> Everyone committed to the organization should know the mission statement by heart because it is the reason the organization exists and is the basis of people's commitment to the organization. (Angelica 2001, 18)

The vision statement delineates what a company wants to be in the future (three to five years).

> A good vision statement inspires and challenges the board, staff, and volunteers without overwhelming them—they must believe they can accomplish it. (Angelica 2001, 21)

Policies and procedures both are derived and instituted from the mission and vision statements to ensure that the mission and vision statements are achieved. Policies are guidelines used to set the direction of every organization, while procedures are routine steps that organizations steadily follow to attain the result.

> Policies and procedures provide decision makers with limits, alternatives, and general guidelines. They help to make instructions definite, provide a common understanding of a policy interpretation, and provide quick settlement of misunderstanding. (Page 2006, 8)

All policies and procedures must be connected with the laws of the state in which the company or organization is located. Most importantly, they must be aligned with God's morals and values. No one can run a company effectively without having these declarations in place; employees need to master these declarations after they are hired. This applies to mom-and-pop businesses as well. If a small business doesn't have such declarations in place, wouldn't it be great if you developed them? On the other hand, it's one thing to have these declarations and another to enforce them effectively. Enforcing them will strengthen and grow your business.

Companies that enforce these declarations, however, won't avoid challenges, and those that don't enforce them still will have challenge. It doesn't matter; you will face fate at some point. It will knock at your door without notice. Whether a company enforces these declarations or not, they will face multiple challenges in the workplace, which may or may not create an opportunity to adjust their mission and vision statements.

Look at every challenge as an opportunity instead of going south with it. Challenges will occur in all aspects of life, as well as the workplace; they should be expected with a plan intact. These challenges can range from minor to extreme issues and could be costly. To prevent such a dilemma, expect the unexpected and have safety plans to combat these circumstances.

It is important to stay humble with whatever you do. Each organization must ensure that their policies and procedures are consistently and effectively implemented in order to dodge or avoid as many disasters as possible. When the business takes a negative turn, people within and outside the company will bring ten thousand and one ideas to your attention. These people may be looking at the here and now. Great leaders or organizations must listen to those ideas, but they should not focus on instant gratification; they should analyze those ideas thoroughly and identify how the idea would impact them in the long term.

Some unforeseen challenges brought by fate can be frustrating and annoying; they might create self-doubt or even lead someone to quit or the business to close. Put God first in your life and before those missions, visions, policies, and procedures; otherwise, it will be impossible to make it through.

Commit to the Lord whatever you do, and He will establish your plans. (Proverbs 16:3)

You must truly understand who you are (your morals and values), but it's also crucial to understand the organization's drive, whether you are employer or employee. If you're a potential employee, research the organization by visiting its website. Ask the right questions and process all feedback thoroughly. You also must ensure that the organization's morals and values do not violate yours.

As I was processing this section in my mind, I wondered if a few people working at different companies could define their companies' missions and visions. I wondered how many of them would remember. Business owners will find it attractive if you master the company declarations, and they are more likely to trust you and move you up the ladder.

I would not be surprised if some members of an organization do not know that their company has a website. It is very beneficial to ask questions. Not every business can afford to maintain a website or have access to resources like big companies do, but it is beneficial to start with what you have at that moment. If you focus on God's morals and values, develop your mission and vision statements, and abide by your state's laws, your business will grow; if you're the employee, you will grow at the company you work for.

These declaration statements are not just for show. You should consistently remind yourself that they were put in place to help keep you in line and help you to succeed. It would be beneficial to review the mission and vision statements and the policies and procedures of the company every quarter to ensure the goals and objectives are being met and progressing. If you do, your employer will take you more seriously, and that could lead to personal growth within the company. As mentioned, reviewing them could lead to adjustments to what you have already as you expand. Everyone who works for a company, including owners and employees, should be able to adhere to the policies and procedures that govern them.

We must acknowledge that there are personal struggles or distractions around us that may result in our paying less attention at work or to our growth there. The one and only remedy is to stay focused and lean on God always. Without focusing on and leaning on Him, it could be the end of your career pursuit, and you could find yourself in a vicious work cycle.

I can do all things through Him who gives me strength. (Philippians 4:13)

Pregraduation Practicum and Internship Experiences

Going to college is great, but not everyone is meant to succeed through education. That said, all colleges and universities provide their students with pregraduation practicum and internship experiences. Transitioning from a knowledge-based atmosphere (in class lectures) to a practical-based atmosphere (field work) can be very challenging to potential graduates. This is where the rubber (classroom experiences) meets the road (field work experiences). It may feel like you don't fit in at first, but sometimes, we have to be patient. Ask for strength and understanding from God. Some circumstances are expected and should be embraced. In fact, this should be your best opportunity to study and learn that company's mission, vision, policies, and procedures. Doing so will help you establish a solid foundation for yourself.

Even though many colleges and universities provide their students with practicum and internship opportunities at a company of their choice, some people find it difficult to find a company at which they can intern within a short time.

We live in a world of technology. I know of students who could not find a place to complete their pregraduation experiences, which resulted in their seeking out-of-state organizations, which meant they could only participate virtually. I feel that's not the same, although some people would say otherwise. Still, I would suggest that you participate live, instead of from the comfort of your home, in order to acquire as much as you can. Technology is great with certain careers but not for all. Practicums and internships can feel rushed. This does not apply to every student, as some students are blessed in securing an organization that provides great training for them. Some practicums and internships require many hours to complete, and they appear to be a struggle. In some cases, by the time the students settle down and start learning the most crucial aspects of that business or the field they studied, it's almost time for them to submit their hours for graduation. No college or university wants their students to graduate with minimal experience, even though they are guaranteed to graduate. This could be a concern for many students who may not be confident to speak up about it. Every intern should gather as much information about the organization as possible in order to understand its "drive" in order to succeed.

You can access those documents online, and some companies have printed copies in their offices for your review.

A few years ago, I supervised an intern student whose only focus was to see clients. He couldn't wait to get into the field and appeared to be very impatient while I was educating him on the company's vision, mission, policies, and procedures. I explained the benefits of understanding each document and advised him to review the documents privately in order to understand what he was getting into.

An intern's attitude toward these documents could decide if the intern is a good fit and if he or she can make it through. If he or she doesn't want to learn how to swim before diving headfirst, it may not be a pretty scene. The reason for interning is to gain the most experience possible in the field the person has chosen.

You may find out that your chosen career is not what you really want to do. There is nothing wrong with that. If you are a slow learner like me, and you want to learn as much as possible, take your time. Don't rush through it. If a person is not well grounded, he or she could face even more challenges and could fail. Will the process of learning these steps be boring, frustrating, or annoying? Possibly, but it would be in your best interest to do so.

Developing a Résumé (Curriculum Vitae)

A résumé or curriculum vitae contains your complete educational background and work experience. When some hear about the educational component, they tend to view it as useless. This could be the reason that some people do not care to develop a résumé and have it handy. Developing a résumé is very attractive to employers. It doesn't matter what type of job you are applying for. An employer who has never met you will see you through your résumé. Even if you interned at an organization that adored you, you still should have a résumé. It's not guaranteed that you will be working for that same company after graduation. Through your résumé, the employer will decide if it's worth his or her time to invite you for an interview. If you don't have much experience for the job you are applying for, be honest about it. Don't feel ashamed, as you must start somewhere.

Honesty can get you the job when you have fewer experiences on your résumé, but you need to pray and commit everything to God's hands. If it's His will, you will get that job. If not, keep trying, and a better one will show up.

Dan Clay, author of *How to Write the Perfect Resume*, offers the following information:

> There's no shortage of information out there covering how to write a better resume–just google "resume writing tips" and you'll see nearly 3 million pages of search results! With so many sources of advice and recommendations, you'd think everyone's resume would be perfect by now, right? Think again. (...) One study found that for every job a company posts, it receives 250 resumes. Of these, only one will be offered the job. That's a 99.6% failure rate among those who submitted their resume—more than adequate to define the status quo. (2018, 5)

I suggest visiting your local career center for face-to-face assistance. I am a very slow learner and always do better with someone educating me in person, rather than learning online. Don't be ashamed or embarrassed. Always update your résumé when you change jobs, and review it with someone you trust. Do not wait until the last minute because being under pressure—even mild pressure—could lead to mistakes and disqualifications.

Some organizations may not be interested in your résumé but may call you in to complete their employment application or ask you to do so through their website. In that case, you have enough time to ensure you do not make any mistakes. Employers pick up on things that do not add up and will question you if they are really interested in you. If it's a hard copy of an employment application, grab more than one copy. Grab three or more, if necessary. The employer could be assessing your handwriting and your ability to write. As I said, I am a very slow learner who has ADHD and dyslexia. It took me some time to realize that every time I write anything down, I tend to make a mistake, and I don't do well where there are distractions. Now that I know how I operate, I grab more than one document in case I make a mistake. You might want to do the same. Even if you are a great writer, I still recommend that you grab more than one application form. Remember, first appearances matter, and someone may assess your personality type from looking at a piece of paper. Stay humble, and don't get too confident because whatever you submit could belong to the 99.6 percent who never call. If you are not sure of a question on the application, consult with someone you trust. Avoid making up an answer because that could be the only question the employer will ask you that you are not prepared to answer. Then, you might not be called at all.

Preparing for an Interview

To some, preparing for an interview can be very stressful. You must figure out what to wear; review the content of your résumé or curriculum vitae, not knowing what they will ask; and figure out the location of the job interview so you won't be late. Some people arrive but are sweating so bad that they look dramatic. Many years ago, I was excited about an interview, but I also was anxious at the same time because I didn't know how the interview would go. I woke up at 6:00 a.m., as the appointment was at 9:00. When I left that morning, I drove in the wrong direction for about forty-five minutes without realizing it. I let my anxiety rip me apart that morning. I was thankful to God, however, that I made it there on time. That was a rough morning, but I got the job.

I was asked how tall I was, out of the blue, and my response was to give my weight. The interviewer laughed and called me a joker, but I wondered why. My point? Leave as early as possible. Expect some drama to occur in the process. Be there at least fifteen to thirty minutes early. The interviewer should not be waiting on you. You should be waiting on the interviewer. Try not to be there too early, however, unless you intend to participate in a staring contest. Always make sure to check in so the interviewer knows you are there. Pray about it, and ask others you trust to pray for you as well. Let God lead the way. Depending on the type of job, practice or rehearse questions and answers with someone.

Make sure your résumé or whatever documents they've requested are up-to-date. Make your reference sources aware of your job application and the possibility that the organization could call them. Get enough rest before the interview, and don't overdress. Overdressing could be a turnoff, depending on the type of job you are seeking.

The interviewer may ask if you have a criminal record. I would suggest that you make it known, whatever that is. Do not let them find that out on their own. It may seem embarrassing at that moment, but being honest could secure you the job. Avoid talking too much. Make your responses simple and straight to the point. You don't want the interviewer to fall asleep on you or get agitated by lengthy answers. The amount of time you speak could determine the length of your interview. Maintain appropriate posture and eye contact, but don't stare at the interviewer. Monitor his or her body language. If you answer any question incorrectly and you realize you did, correct your statement because the organization may have already researched you thoroughly prior to the interview.

All your social media activities may come into play. So your morals and values could come into play as well. The interviewer could put you on the spot by presenting scenarios and questions on how you would react to each scenario. If you are not sure, say that you are not sure. Leave all your prior problems or conflicts at the door. Do not take them with you, as they could backfire. Regardless of what your personality type is, even if you consider that position an excellent fit, leave your ego at home. Remember that pride goes before a fall (Proverbs 16:18).

Sometimes during the interview, an employer will ask if you have any questions. Ask what drives their company and what their mission and vision are. Don't assume you know it all—doing so may be interpreted as your not being a very good candidate. Have a notepad and pen with you to write things down, if necessary. You have the right to ask questions about salary. If you found the job online or had a lead, thoroughly review the content, as some of your questions may also stem from the advertisement.

A reference letter is completed by a sponsor on behalf of an applicant. It is a positive seal of approval of the applicant's abilities and attributes. It comments on the applicant's positive skills and attributes, but it must look neat and professional. Every document requested by a potential employer could determine if you are hired or not hired. I think some people take the "formats" the employers request for granted. Some of the reference letters I have read do not have signatures on them. They were well-typed letters of reference, but having no signature made them look weak and unattractive. Expect the employer to reject it, as it could have been written by anyone. Some employers may contact the person after receiving his or her reference letter because they need to know that the person is legitimate. Also, the employer may ask questions based on the reference letter. Therefore, be careful who you select to complete references.

Do not ever take a snapshot of a reference letter or a reference form and send it to an employer. I view that as a turnoff. Before you submit the reference letter, complete the form and make sure it meets the employer's requirements. Some who write reference letters leave some sections blank or write N/A in those sections. If you are asking past employers to write a letter of recommendation for you, make sure it is written on their letterheads. Everyone is in a rush nowadays. When anything is rushed, however, it looks like something you dragged out from the mud. Remember that first impressions matter. I have observed some references presented to an employer that looked folded about ten thousand times. Some had coffee stains on them.

If you are anxious for any reason, take advantage of the local career center. There are a lot of things I do not know about, but I am not ashamed or embarrassed to ask questions. Ask questions if you are not sure. You can also get clarification from the employer's human resources to ensure you are submitting the requested documents properly.

You may have already known some of what I disclosed to you. Maybe you have other thoughts you can add to it or subtract. Some may assume this information refers to large corporations, but mom-and-pop shops, restaurants, and so forth are included. Even if it's a family business, it's advisable to do the same. Take whatever you are doing seriously because your growth and progress depend on it. Remember—avoid putting God on the back burner. With Him, all things are possible (Matthew 19:26).

Mom-and-pop shops should consider the above recommendations. Remember that you will get traction based on how you portray your business. If you portray it as mediocre, you will attract mediocre. If you portray it as a serious business and set a decent bar, then you will attract serious and decent applicants. Since mom-and-pop shops and other small businesses are family-oriented, it is beneficial to ask applicants about their families and relationships. It doesn't matter if the applicant is from a broken home or a home with both parents. How applicants respond to these questions may reveal a lot to you without their saying a lot. Remember—you won't know unless you ask questions. You may end up inspiring someone who's applying from a broken home. He or she needs to start somewhere, and working for you may be the best thing that has ever happened in his or her life.

Regardless of how big or small the company is, they may require a second interview with you for a follow-up question or to offer you the job. That's a very good sign. In fact, it can go either way. If the job is offered to you, congratulations. If not, you will probably be torn or disappointed. Some companies may send you an email, letter in the mail, or meet you face-to-face to encourage you, even though the job was not offered to you; sometimes, there will be no contact at all.

Some will inform you they will make their decision within forty-eight to seventy-two hours but may not do so at all. That might be a sign that you were not hired. But then, they may contact you to offer you the job, which is your fate and destiny at work. I believe that whatever the case may be, God works in mysterious ways. If the job is not offered to you, that job was not meant for you. Whoever the job was meant for will get the position. Some companies prefer to hire someone who is inexperienced so they can train the candidate in the way they want. It might go the other way as well. You just never know.

Whatever the outcome is, don't give up. It doesn't feel good to get rejected. Keep searching, and something much more suitable for you will be unveiled before your sight. Remember that some organizations may require you to complete an aptitude test or personality test to conclude your interview. Expect that to be presented to you. Hiring processes can be very exhausting. The organization needs to make sure you are an excellent fit.

First Week Expectations and Trainings

The first week of work should be about training. I once worked for a company that required a week's training before they would assign me some responsibilities. At first, I thought it was a waste of their resources and manpower, since I was being paid. Later, I realized that it was in my best interest and the company's best interest to better comprehend the company's stance and what drives them. The one-week training was the best thing that ever happened to me because it helped make me who I am today. The company was Neighbor to Family, located in Daytona Beach, Florida. Other companies that contributed to my growth were the House Next Door in Deland, Florida, and Circle of Friends Services in Deltona, Florida. Training was offered not only the first week on the job but on a frequent basis. It was worth the time and effort, and I will never forget how much they helped me.

Since then, I have encouraged my colleagues to always keep their minds open and focused to absorb as much as they can during any training, as this can determine how they grow with a company. Some companies may conduct training quarterly, every six months, or yearly. Any training-related activities should include learning the vision and mission statements and the policies and procedures of the company. Making a profit is paramount for every company, but helping employees understand how their policies and procedures are connected to this objective will solidify their ability and understanding to get the job done appropriately.

If you attain a job and you are not trained well, you have been set up to fail. If that is the case, you will feel frustrated and hate the job and could be on the verge of losing your job. During training times, bring up issues you may have encountered that were favorable or unfavorable; this could be a teachable moment for your colleagues. While doing so, don't forget to listen, take notes, or even record the training. Some trainers will provide you with a transcript of the training and other resources as well. Some of the training may or may not require a quiz.

A Chinese proverb says, "Give a man a fish, and you will feed him for a day. Teach a man to fish, and you will feed him for a lifetime" (Tripp 1970, 96). Companies need to cover all aspects of training for the new employees to build confidence and knowledge about their drive. Remember that the amount of time spent on training your employees can determine how great they will be and how long they will last. Assuming that a new employee is educated and understands what needs to be done could be a regrettable mistake. Each company is different and runs differently. It's imperative to educate the employee on how the operation is run. These recommendations also apply to mom-and-pop shops and other small businesses.

Providing adequate training for all employees falls on the employer, not the employees. Providing training costs money and time, but it's something that must be done. There should be a budget and a plan in place to keep growing or flourishing. Providing as little training as possible to save some money may end up costing you more in the long run. Remember—it's the employer's responsibility to ensure that the employees are equipped to do their jobs.

Contract work takes a different approach, as the contract workers will be responsible for covering their own training. New employees should not just learn how to produce goods and services for profit purposes but also should understand how to effectively align the company's policies and procedures while they are doing so. After all, the employers will reap most of the benefits.

Even though some people may be intelligent from a knowledge-based point of view, applying that knowledge or turning that knowledge into practice could be challenging to some. Employers should expect this kind of challenge. Remember that everyone has a different personality, and they learn differently. What may take Mr. A. two days to grasp may take Mr. B. seven days to grasp. As I've mentioned, I am a very slow learner, and it took me a long time to master concepts. It took me some time to come to terms with this, but I feel very good about myself now. If this sounds like you, you should not be ashamed of it. Just never give up. Training should not be one-size-fits-all and should accommodate different personalities in order to achieve the best and lasting result.

Dealing with Work Stress or Burnout

Many different activities happen in a workplace. I suggest that you stay focused on what you are asked to do, as there will be a lot of distractions.

Burnout has become rampant in almost every workplace. Many of the people I spoke to regarding how they felt about their jobs complained about burnout. What does burnout mean? It can be defined as a physical or mental breakdown caused by overwork. When someone is in the burnout zone, the person is under extreme stress. Burnout may trigger many negative outcomes, including mistakes or errors. If that is the case, health issues may result from the extreme stress.

Some people described how much they loved their careers but felt they were overloaded. What their work used to be and what it is today is like night and day. Reasons they listed included limited manpower to do the job, budget cuts to save money, and the manager trusting no one but them to get the job done properly. Many of these employees were promised promotions or recognition for their skills with bonuses, but none of them received the promotion or bonus. In some cases, they were given a pat on the back or a certificate instead. Those gestures won't pay their bills.

It is not fair to make empty promises to your best employees. Some arrive at work very early and are the last to leave. Some do not complain at all, even though their family members have complained about their absence. We need to determine when an employee is used to attain an objective that favors the employer but not the employee. The sad part is that some of these employees refuse to say anything to their managers because they think they will lose their positions if they make their voices heard regarding raises, bonuses, or promotions. Under which circumstances can someone speak up and not face negative consequences?

Many companies have suggestion boxes in their offices, but I do not have confidence that it is effective. If someone is doing the best job for a company, the company does not need a suggestion box to be told the employee needs to be promoted or rewarded. There are staff meetings, face-to-face meetings with supervisors, and quarterly and annual evaluations. Employees should feel confident in speaking up without having to go through suggestion boxes. Then again, most companies have an open-door policy, but some employees see that as a make-believe open-door policy. If it's an open-door policy, why are some employees afraid to walk into their manager's office? It distances employers from their employees, rather than bringing them closer together.

Not only are there burnout-related issues in the workplace, but there are also competitions and interpersonal situations going on as well. After speaking to a few people about interpersonal conflicts at their jobs, most reported that the nature of those conflicts was very silly. One, however, stood out. This one was a competition. There is nothing wrong with employees competing to increase revenue or pay, but competition should be guarded by the rules and regulations that govern that company. It is very easy for humans to deviate from the policies and procedures of the company and focus on their self-centered desires. Also, it is very easy for humans to err during challenges like these. It's the manager's responsibility to ensure that everyone stays in line. Never choose politics over policies.

Sometimes, it is easy for managers to be triangulated into these conflicts without being aware, which may cause low morale, self-serving frustrations, employee stress, and lower production. Then, the company focuses on the problem or conflict its employees are having instead of the production of goods and services for their customers. If proper steps are not taken, the situation could get worse and could drain the life of the company. A manager who cannot be effective and make impartial decisions in the best interest of the company is part of the problem.

Employees always know where their managers stand in how they relate to their employees. The objective of a manager is to model the behaviors he or she expects to see in the workplace. One of the employees' goals is to get the manager on their side as much as possible, but the manager's goal is to stay consistent with meeting the objectives of the company, not the employees, regardless of whether he or she is liked.

As a manager, it's your responsibility to manage employees with different personalities in your workplace, but it's also your responsibility to ensure they are managed through your company's policies and procedures. Managing employees with different personalities is very challenging. Therefore, each company establishes different but interrelated practice guides to ensure it's less challenging. It is normal to make unprecedented decisions when facing interpersonal conflicts, but they should be geared toward favoring the company, instead of a person, in order to maintain a stable and healthy work environment.

After speaking to a few people from different agencies, I learned that some of these interpersonal conflicts were created by their management. Sometimes, management can create a competitive atmosphere because that is what's best for business. This can happen because there wasn't proper planning or because they failed to consider the consequences. We tend to forget the human-nature aspect of things and forget to take into consideration how aggressive humans can get when in competition.

Some competitive efforts are innocently introduced in order to raise revenues, but if proper care is not taken, it can turn into a nightmare. Instead of retrieving, taking responsibility, and implementing necessary or effectively corrective action plans, they reprimand their employees. Failure to align new ideas to your company's policies and procedures can be harmful to you, as the manager, and the employees. Many beneficial resources can be incorporated with a company's policies and procedures to help increase revenues and keep employees happy, and those resources, when executed or implemented appropriately, result in a win/win situation. It's human nature to compete, regardless of who wins or loses in the end. In order to become effective in managing others, one must understand human behavior in order to understand what drives people individually.

Another workplace challenge that many people face is bullying. Bullying has become one of the most destructive forces around the world. The sad part is that the person being bullied may not have anywhere to go and may choose to tolerate it because of a paycheck. I wish bullying could be contained, but it was here before I was born and will most likely be here after I am gone. It will continue to occur in all aspects of life, and many people choose to stay quiet about the abuse. Yes, it also occurs in workplaces between managers and their employees or vice versa. When bullying occurs in a workplace, harassment may occur as well. It's not attractive in any way, shape, or form.

Employee manuals, policies, and procedures generally don't address bullying, but regardless of the situation, abuse of power is never acceptable. Can you imagine getting up in the morning and becoming overwhelmed by anxiety symptoms because your manager despises you, and you feel that you could lose your job in the blink of an eye as a result? Some employees are overlooked for promotions or do not get the raises they deserve, and there is nothing they can do about it. Finding a good-paying job elsewhere is not an option, and they're doing the best they can to hang on to what they have now. They can't even go to their manager's superior, as they're afraid he or she will side with the manager who's abusing them. One of the most devastating forms of abuse is emotional or mental. Many employees experience bullying and abuse of all kinds.

Imagine if the bullying stopped. Employee morale would improve, which would result in an increase in production and services. Bullies undermine the policies, procedures, and success of a company. But what is the intention of the bully? It's to show power and control and to sabotage the progress of his business. Why would their superiors stand by and do nothing to help those employees serving them? There must be underlying issues from the person's past that would lead someone to consistently bully his or her employees.

Companies face many issues. These issues are better resolved diplomatically than with bullying. Anyone who uses bullying to settle a score with an employee lacks leadership skills and should not be in a position of leadership. That person does not belong there and should be terminated or else that company will suffer unimaginably one day. Some managers have no filter and are extremely inconsiderate; in most cases, they feel they are indispensable. There is no reason whatsoever to bully those who are working under them.

I have worked at many different companies over the years and am very thankful I was never discriminated against by any employer. All the companies I worked for treated me with respect and dignity, regardless of who I was. Not everyone, however, has that privilege. Discrimination in the workplace does exist, and many people suffer beyond measure as a result. It's like the silent killer at the workplace.

Every company has an employee manual, policies, and procedures that it follows, and all have a clause that states that employers can't discriminate based on race, gender, religion, national origin, physical or mental disability, age, sexual orientation, or gender identity. So why do some employers choose to ignore this? If the company's mission and vision are to succeed, why engage in activities that would sabotage it? It's unfortunate that many employees who deserve to be promoted and get raises are prevented from reaching their goals because they are discriminated against.

Every company wants to be represented by the best, but wouldn't it be impossible for anyone to be at his or her best if he or she is discriminated against? Discrimination can occur at any time. Imagine if we could interview employers and get the honest answers for why they disqualified an applicant who applied for a position at their companies. Some are not even letting applicants in the door to be interviewed, but what if the person an employer overlooked was someone who could have been the best fit?

A Job is a privilege. Millions of people would like to be in the workforce or want to have the position you have today at your workplace. Unfortunately, some employees take their positions for granted, but how could that be? Could it be that some are arrogant or feel self-entitled or irreplaceable? Even those who are tenured in certain areas of expertise act as though they are above the law and can never be terminated. This is false. Nothing is guaranteed, regardless of who you are or how close you are to management. Is it permissible for someone to believe these thoughts about himself or herself because that person is doing his or her job excellently and going above and beyond for the company? Yes, that person deserves to feel arrogant, entitled, and irreplaceable, as long as it doesn't go to his or her head, as that person has consistently proven how solidly he or she is engraved in the company's policies and procedures and has shown full commitment to them. Many companies love employees who are loyal, have self-respect, are committed, and take pride in their work. These companies are willing to go above and beyond to preserve those who take their work seriously on a regular basis.

Remember, if you continue to do your job as expected or beyond expectations, your company will do its part for you in return.

We need to teach our employees how we want to be treated. If we treat them right, they will return the favor.

There are great employees, but, unfortunately, there are bad ones as well. There will always be that "one." Some employees cannot justify why they feel arrogant, irreplaceable, or entitled. It's just in their heads, and they do not possess the ability to be honest with themselves. Some people regularly mischaracterize themselves and cannot back up who or what they claim to be. They have difficulty comprehending who they are and who they think they are. They should be worried, and if they are not, then there is something wrong with that picture.

Some of the firestorms created in the workplace today are inflicted by some employees. Some recognize the issues and adjustments they need to make but fail to do so. Very few are motivated to do something about the situation or to take necessary steps to rise above matters.

I speak to strangers everywhere I go; maybe that's because I am very approachable and love every opportunity. I get to help people at any time and anywhere. Some cannot understand that their negative attitudes or behaviors, lack of commitment to their positions, or lack of motivation toward their employers or their positions could be preventing them from moving up the ladder, like others who succeeded in doing. Some of the strangers I've spoken to in the past felt as if their lives were cursed because they were not in the position they desired at their workplaces and felt they would never get there.

While I was on my way to Ireland for my nephew's wedding, I met a middle-aged man who was on a business trip from Canada. Within minutes, we touched upon what we each did for a living. When I asked if he loved his job, it took him a couple of seconds to respond, and he appeared as if he was going to cry.

"It's OK to take your time," I told him. "You don't have to answer if you don't want to."

"No, I can," he said, and he described in detail what he did at his job. He described it so amazingly that I immediately thought he would be fun to work with. Then he said, "I love my job, but I don't like the people who manage it or the policies and procedures they have in place. My managers are overly demanding, as each employee must meet a certain quota to maintain their positions and maintain the resources flowing into their position. Marketing is not easy, but I would not trade it for anything else. What hurts me the most is that I could have been one of their vice presidents and gotten a raise, but I didn't because I haven't been getting along with my superiors."

"What do you mean by not getting along?" I asked.

"I argue with my superiors on a frequent basis and don't accept certain assignments from them. I'm late to work sometimes, but I feel I should be treated differently from others because I've been there longer than anyone else."

He went on to describe feeling irritable, not very happy, depressed, hard on himself, and anxious about his future, even though he appeared to have everything together in his life. Even though he felt things were basically OK, he sensed he could lose his position there.

I listened to him and reflected on the important things he mentioned. Then I informed him that I was glad he was feeling depressed, anxious, and irritable. He immediately gave me a look as if he was about to lose his mind, but thankfully, he allowed me to explain. I said, "It seems you're having difficulty acculturating into your company's ways of operating, even though you've been there for several years. You need to put your ego aside and embrace the experiences at your job in order to get your goals and objectives met. Do you think that things at your job might start to look up if you make some changes?"

I explained that his approaches had not worked in his favor, and he would need to embrace his workplace policies and procedures, as well as respect his superiors, regardless of who they were. Why continue to implement steps that left him feeling miserable and prevented him from climbing up the ladder? If he wanted to move up, then respecting and complying with his superiors and following through with his company's policies and procedures shouldn't get in his way.

Even though he knew better, I explained what employers look for in an employee, such as someone who's not divisive. What if his superiors thought he was not a good fit for management or didn't deserve a raise because he was argumentative and noncompliant?

"If you want others to change or make some adjustments," I said, "you must make the adjustments or changes first. Why continue to act in ways that don't favor you?"

He listened and then said, "I was trying to save my company. I tend to be extremely upset or angry when no one listens to my ideas. Now I understand that I'm holding myself back." He then made a promise to himself that he would follow through by adjusting.

We exchanged business cards, and I am looking forward to hearing from him in the future about his progress.

Picture this in your mind: This man is very talented and should be well respected. He has worked for years for a marketing company and thought he was doing the right things, even though he hadn't earned the result he deserved. This man believed that his aggressive approaches would earn him a promotion, but he had no clue that he was ruffling his superiors' feathers. Shouldn't he have detected these problems from his annual evaluations, or didn't the company inform him of the areas in which he struggled? Can you imagine being in a position where you thought that great things were happening at your job and that your superiors loved your approaches, maybe because you had not been let go, and then you found out they were planning how to get rid of you? Be careful. You may think you have everything in control, but your superiors may be reviewing résumés for your replacement because they feel your behavior is inappropriate. Never take your work privilege for granted.

Don't let your ego get in your way, and don't take years to realize your approaches are not working out for you. Employers appreciate employees who work hard and have great ideas, but they also appreciate those who simply comply with the company's way of running their business. You must learn to acculturate yourself into the company's policies and procedures, whether you like it or not.

There was a reason that gentleman and I crossed paths on the plane. Maybe he needed to hear that the symptoms he was experiencing were normal, and since he did not like them, he would need to make some changes to get a better outcome. At least he stayed at the same job, even though it took him all these years to start making changes. Some employees jump from one job to another throughout their careers, thinking issues will go away, although the issues stem from their own behaviors. If you have done this, realize the problem likely is you, not the companies you worked for. The only constant is you. Try to pinpoint the problem within you instead of pointing fingers at the management.

Another challenge people face at their workplaces is conflict within management or leadership. If management is not healthy, then its employees will not be healthy. It's unfortunate that employees suffer because the leadership cannot get its act together. Some employees are confused, not knowing to whom they should listen or how to proceed with their assignments. In some cases, the management is so unhealthy that it reaches the point of the tail wagging the dog—and that is not a good thing for business.

Being a member of the management sometimes gets into people's heads, and they forget the reason they were there to lead. What are the sources of the struggles within the management? Could it be that some are there to serve themselves? Some bring personal issues to work, and some aren't cooperative with others. Some suffer from narcissism, harmful competition, overload, unhealthy lifestyles, and personality conflicts. Most often, when you find out what's causing division among the leaders or management of a company, they have made mountains out of molehills. Most situations can be considered ridiculous.

Should everyone in leadership be perfect? Not at all, but everyone in leadership should strive for excellence. You are not likely to be in tune with others when you're striving for excellence versus perfection. Things usually will go wrong when someone in management does not uphold, model, and enforce the policies and procedures of the company that he or she leads.

When someone in management is asked what their mission and vision statements are, it's sad if they cannot say, but they can tell you how many times someone else in management rubbed them the wrong way. As a manager, failing to pursue priorities that are in the best interests of your company could result in disaster for your subordinates.

The above factors mentioned can make the workplace strenuous. We do have some control over these issues if we make more of an effort to follow the company's guidelines, such as the policies and procedures. We can never go wrong by doing so. Providing necessary training at necessary times will empower employees and keep everyone up-to-date.

Graduating students should not wait until the last minute to apply for internship positions but should seek them years before their graduation to ensure that they are choosing the right company to train and equip them for the outside world. They should remember that they may be hired for their good work at that same company.

Regardless of where you are or what you're seeing, hearing, and doing, you will face many challenges, which I believe everyone should expect and embrace. Human beings can problem-solve regardless of the situation.

Our workplace is our second home. It is a privilege and should be considered as such. Why do we neglect that which is of great value to us? Can you imagine how a workplace would look if everyone acknowledged each other's personality differences? Can you imagine how our workplaces would be if we kept focused on the company's goals and objectives instead of our own? We are there for the company's interests, not our own.

Can you imagine what a workplace would look like if management provided necessary resources and training, rewarded the overworked employees as they should, didn't bully their subordinates, and didn't discriminate? Every employee and employer would be enthusiastic. I have witnessed many employees and employers who left work and still had their badges on, regardless of the position the person held. Without your part, the company would not be successful. If you want to be treated with respect at work, be respectful. If you love what you do and want to be promoted or earn bonuses, do what's necessary instead of shooting yourself in the foot. Let your mind think it, but let your actions advocate for it.

Nothing can prevent you from reaching your dream, except you. If you feel that you are too good to do your job appropriately, then you don't deserve to work there. Follow three simple guidelines: (1) stay consistent with your company's policies and procedures, (2) treat your employees well to reach your objectives, and (3) encourage employees to do the same to receive well-deserved rewards. Regardless of the position you hold, always contribute to making your workplace safe, both physically and emotionally.

CHAPTER 4

SPIRITUAL TYPE AND PATHWAY

I recommend that you listen to this song as it's relevant to this chapter's theme, "He Shall Reign Forevermore" by Chris Tomlin

Major Events Before Christ Came

Prior to Christ's arriving on earth, a series of events occurred, as recorded in the Old Testament. I have chosen a few that stood out to me; there may be others that stand out to you. This is a synopsis of where God is coming from. To find out more, I encourage you to read your Bible; it is very healthy to do so.

God intends for us to prosper (past, present, and future) beyond measure. How do I know this? Because He made us in His image. Second, He gave us dominion over everything (Genesis 1:26–30). I am not sure what else we could ask for. God gave Adam and Eve one instruction (Genesis 2:16). Then, obedience was breached (Genesis 3). There was only one instruction to obey.

Adam lived for 930 years. Because the wickedness of the human race increased, God regretted that He had made human beings on earth, and His heart was very troubled. Then, there was a flood during Noah's lifetime. Water flooded the earth for 150 days (Genesis 6–8). Again, God hit the reset button to start fresh and blessed Noah the way He'd blessed Adam (Genesis 9). Noah lived 950 years.

Don't forget that due to one sin, we went from being immortal to mortal (Genesis 6:3). Have you noticed that life expectancy massively dropped from nine hundred–plus to one hundred–plus? Many could barely make it to one hundred now.

Notice that God blessed Adam by saying,

> Be fruitful and increase in number; fill the earth and subdue it. Rule over the fish of the sea and the birds of the air and over every living that moves on the ground. (Genesis 1:28)

After the reset button, God gave Noah the same blessing:

> The God blessed Noah and his sons, saying to them, be fruitful and increase in number and fill the earth. My conclusion, God wanted us to fill the earth and multiply. But humans had a different plan instead of God's plan. So, in a human's mind, being fruitful, increasing and filling the earth was a bad, bad idea. Rather than taking God's route, they chose to build a tower to the heavens in order to stay together. (Genesis 11)

Abraham came into the picture, and God made a covenant with him—the first covenant God made with humans. God revealed to Adam that his descendants would be strangers in another country, enslaved, and mistreated for four hundred years. God vowed to rescue them (Genesis 15). God promised Abraham a son, and that promise was fulfilled at age one hundred. During Abraham's lifetime, God visited Sodom and Gomorrah to find out if their sins were serious. It was evident that their sin was "grievous." So God destroyed both with burning sulfur (Genesis 18–19).

Let's fast-forward. The story of how Abraham's descendants became strangers who were enslaved and mistreated was set in motion through Joseph (Genesis37). That prophecy came to fruition (Exodus 1). Soon, Moses was introduced, and he played a significant role in rescuing Israelites from their misery (Exodus 2–15). God performed many miracles while they were in transition to the promised land, but Israelites complained through the process. Then God handed down the Ten Commandments to Moses at Mount Sinai (Genesis 10).

I paused and said, "Wow!" Humans could not handle one rule or command with these four promises: "Fruitful, increase, fill, and subdue." How were they going to handle the Ten Commandments? I first thought they were not mature enough to handle ten. Then, I thought they had been exposed to the knowledge of good and evil tracing back to Adam, who ate the fruit from the tree of knowledge of good and evil, which God had instructed them not to eat (Genesis 3). In addition, they were exposed to idols and other grievous sins that God despised in Egypt. So they were mature enough. Therefore, the Ten Commandments had to be established and enforced. There was no other way but to set firm and clear laws and boundaries by which Israelites must abide (Exodus 19–20). They began to operate under God's leadership and guidelines, with responsibilities distributed within them. The goal was to keep their focus on God by obeying and worshiping Him "only," in order to live prosperous lives (Exodus 21–40).

To fast-forward again, the good, bad, and ugly happened between the books of Leviticus and Malachi. For the first time, the Israelites asked for a king. God felt rejected, but He proceeded to give them what they wanted

(1 Samuel 8–10). Later on, David came into the picture and defeated Goliath (1 Samuel 17). As time progressed, Solomon became the king, and God used him to build and complete the temple of God. The temple was huge and beautiful. And everything was put in its place (1 Kings 5–8). Throughout these events, God's steadfast love for all remained consistent, even though God's chosen ones disappointed Him by sinning from every angle. Many kings came and went. The sins stemming from that one fruit that Adam ate continued to haunt them.

There were times when God let things befall them due to their transgressions, but He always rescued them after teaching them some lessons. Some individuals followed Him successfully. Some succumbed to the pressure of sin. Many were prophets and prophesied against corruption and other sinful acts that God forbade. Many prophets were martyred during that period. They were simply delivering messages from God about His love for them—messages of deliverance, repentance, and judgment—but it went in one ear and out the other.

Then, it became more evident that the Son of Man, Jesus Christ, would come and die for our sins because the sins infested everyone beyond measure.

I welcome you to read the Bible and examine it in order to understand how much God loves us and wants to be close to us, as well as how much He hates sin. His steadfast love for us endures forever.

The Only Ultimate Sacrifice and Spiritual Pathway

"It is finished" (John 19:30).

First, I encourage you to listen to this song as it reminds us how thankful we should feel for the price Christ paid on the cross for us, "Worthy Is the Lamb" by Hillsong and Delirious

> God is on a cross. The Creator of the universe is being executed. Spit and blood are called to His cheeks and His lips are cracked and swollen. Thorns rips His scalp. His lungs scream with pain. His legs knot with cramps. (...) Yet, death is not ready. And there is no one to save Him, for He is sacrificing Himself. It is no normal six hours ... it is no normal Friday. Far worse than the breaking of His body is the shredding of His heart. His own countrymen clamored for His death. His own disciples planted a kiss of betrayal. His friends ran for cover. And now His father is beginning to turn His back on Him, leaving Him alone. A witness could not help but ask: Jesus,

do you give no thought of saving Yourself? What keeps you there? What holds You to the cross? Nails don't hold Gods to trees. What makes you stay? (Lucado 1989, 22)

Read that again!

I have watched movies and shows and have listened to preachers about the death and Resurrection of Christ countless times, but I still did not comprehend enough how cruel and brutal humans can be until I watched *The Passion of the Christ* in 2004. I strongly believe that no human who was abused to that extreme could survive. Even then, I realized that the movie was just a glimpse of what had happened that day.

> The Dialogue that Friday morning was bitter. From the onlookers, "Come down from the cross if you are the Son of God!" From the religious leaders, "He saved others but He can't save himself!" From the soldiers, "If you are the king of Jews, save yourself." Bitter words. Acidic with sarcasm. Wasn't it enough that He was being crucified? Wasn't it enough that he was being shamed as a criminal? Were the nails insufficient? Was the crown of thorns too soft? Had the flogging been too short? For some, apparently so. (Lucado 1986, 23)

A close family friend and I were having a discussion about Jesus's death, and she said, "I understand why He died, but why was it so gruesome?"

I replied, "His death proved how brutal human beings can be."

Now, as I think about it, there was no other way because the way He died was exactly His fate. Jesus Christ's death was and is the one and only death that redeemed each and every one of us from the past, present, and future sins and generations to come until He returns. It was prophesied multiple times by many prophets in the Old Testament about His coming and death.

When babies are born, they are born innocent with pure hearts and no worries or concerns. Can you imagine a newborn baby who knew from the first second He touched down to earth that He was going to die a gruesome death?

> There seems to be a dark side of Christ's life, perhaps due to the realization of the work He came to do. Christ's calling was not a happy one from a human perspective—He came to die. (Jeremiah 1997, 18)

Jesus knew His purpose and fate, but He did not lose sight of either.

> For just as through the disobedience of the one man the many were made sinners, so also through the obedience of the one man the many will be made righteous. (Romans 5:19)

It's crucial that you fully comprehend the significance of Christ's death. Pay attention to the following: While Adam, who made many sinners, lived to be 930 years of age, Christ, who lived for only thirty-three years, rescued us from our sins and made us righteous. Think about the age differences: 930 versus thirty-three. This means that Christ lived only about 4 percent of Adam's life on earth. This demonstrates how crucial and fast-paced his life was but not rushed, for God had a timeline for His one and only Son on earth and didn't have a second to waste.

> I did not even like to tell you of the implications of His wounding. It really means that He was profaned and broken, stained and defiled. He was Jesus Christ when men took him into their evil hands. Soon He was humiliated and profaned. They plucked out His beard. He was stained with His blood, defiled with earth's grime. Yet, he accused no one and He cursed no one. He was Jesus Christ, the wounded One. (Tozer 2009, 87)

Remember in chapter 1, I said that sometimes coded messages or hidden clues are made somewhat visible, even though they can seem blurry at times. We choose to either brush them off, ignore them, or take them for granted. Now, imagine that your tomorrow's fate through God was revealed to you, or you got a glimpse of what would happen to you tomorrow that was not favorable to you. I'd bet you would do everything within your power to avoid, cancel, change, adjust, or prevent that scheduled fate from happening to spare your own life. If it was a favorable revelation, however, of course you would be excited and go with it. Again, why?

That's our human nature. I am absolutely sure we would have ten thousand and one reasons why our lives should be spared. Jesus Christ, from the day of His birth, did not withdraw from His mission because of the certainty of His gruesome death. He forged forward. No one could go through what He went through for one second and live to tell the story.

Prior to Jesus's crucifixion, many senseless attacks and accusations were levied against Him, but He stood tall, regardless.

> He came to that which was His own, but His own did not receive Him. (John 1:11)

Even experts in the Mosaic law (Matthew 22:35; Luke 7:30; 10:25) interrogated and questioned His authority. They were educated enough to twist His words in an attempt to fault and trap Him, but they were not educated enough to know that He wrote the book that they were quoting. These law experts defended the bad and ugly but failed to defend or represent the truth when it counted most. Why? Even though they knew the law, they did not know or recognize Christ as our Savior.

A person could be an expert but lack the Holy Spirit to connect the dots. It was evident that the charges brought against Jesus were senseless. They did not meet either criminal charges or a misdemeanor. In fact, they did not meet any standards or criteria—but that's how God planned it. He was hated because He was and is the Son of God, who came to save us and give us abundant life (John 10:10; 1 Timothy 1:15).

I thought that everyone was presumed innocent until proven guilty. Not in Jesus's case, though. He was presumed guilty from the start. The burden of proof lies with the accusers, but they could not deliver any substantial evidence.

> Burden of proof is the responsibility of producing sufficient evidence in support of a fact or issue and favorably persuading the trier of fact (as a judge or jury) regarding that fact or issue. (Merriam-Webster's *Dictionary of Law* 2011, 6486)

I was reviewing law documents, and it defined the burden of proof in the best and simple way:

> To satisfy its burden of proof, the prosecution must prove all elements of the offense beyond a reasonable doubt. In a murder case, the burden of proof includes showing that the elements which would reduce murder to manslaughter are not present. (Sterling Education 2022, 48)

A review of everything that happened in the last six hours of Christ's life shows a lack of evidence. Pontius Pilate presided over the trial of Jesus. Only Pilate had the power to put Jesus to death. He could not do so because of lack of evidence. Instead of releasing Him, however, the following happened:

> [H]e took water and washed his hands in front of the crowd. I am innocent of this man's blood. It is your responsibility! (Matthew 27:24)

This is not how the judicial system works, but it was Jesus's fate to die a gruesome death without evidence or support.

I thought that since the charges were senseless, one of those experts in Mosaic law would step up to the plate to defend Him. Then I asked myself, "How could they defend someone they despised and didn't understand?" It was His fate that those senseless charges would lead to His crucifixion, which, in turn, led to our redemption and purification from all our sins through His blood.

> But He was pierced for our transgressions, He was crushed for our iniquities; the punishment that brought us peace was on Him, and by His wounds we are healed. (Isaiah 53:5)

Even a criminal who was crucified with Jesus thought it was senseless. If a career criminal could vouch for Jesus, what should prevent us from doing the same? Nothing! Have you noticed that certain things in life do not have to make sense to make sense, as I pointed out in chapter 1? But who were these people who did all this to Him? As humans, we are very good at pointing fingers. How dare you, Judas? How dare you, Pilate? If you think about it, we actually did!

> Let us not eloquently blame Judas, not Pilate. Let us not curl our lips at Judas accuse, "He sold Him for money!" Let us pity Pilate, the weak-willed, because he did not have the courage enough to stand for innocency of the man whom he declared had done no wrong. Let us not curse the Jews for delivering Jesus to be crucified. Let us not single out the Romans in blaming them for putting Jesus on the cross. Oh, they were guilty, certainly! But they were our accomplices in crime. They and we put Him on the cross, not they alone. That rising malice and anger that burns so hotly in your being today puts Him there. (Tozer 1976, 56)

There are so many promises or prophecies that we should acknowledge and accept about Jesus Christ, but I will name three that stand out for me: (1) we must acknowledge and accept that our sinful nature put Jesus on the cross; (2) we must acknowledge and accept that He is our personal Lord and Savior; and (3) we must acknowledge and accept that He will imminently return.

Acknowledgement and Acceptance, Part I

Someone once asked me, "What did I have to do with Jesus's death? I was not born two thousand years ago."

I wondered about that myself and had some difficulty connecting the dots to my playing a role in His death. At first, I felt I was accused of something I did not do. Then, I later came to understand that you and I have been products of sin from the time Adam and Eve got sidetracked from God's one and only instruction:

> And the Lord God commanded the man, you are free to eat from any tree in the garden; but you must not eat from the tree of the knowledge of good and evil, for when you eat it you will certainly die. (Genesis 2:16–17)

But why would God tempt us that way—by having that tree visible and within reach to humans in the first place? Then again, why not? The question can be answered by two terms: obedience and free will. By definition, obedience is simply doing what we are told to do. Free will is an individual's ability to act without restrictions. God did give us above and beyond.

The only thing He requires of us is that we obey Him. God made fire and many other physical things that can harm us. We do not have to be told that playing with fire will burn us. Whenever we use fire, we use it wisely. Imagine what life would be like if we could safeguard the spiritual nature of our beings in the same way as we safeguard our physical nature. So why do we tend to do the things that are not healthy, both spiritually and physically? It's our human nature at work.

I guess when God instructs us not to do a particular thing, we become curious and want to see what would happen if we did what we were asked not to do. Once again, human nature. Remember the saying, "Curiosity killed the cat." That is how we ended up the way we are. Even the apostle Paul acknowledged his weakness and said,

> For I know that good itself does not dwell in me, that is, in my sinful nature. For I have the desire to do what is good, but I cannot carry it out. For I do not do the good I want to do, but evil I do not want to do—this I keep doing. Now if I do what I do not want to do, it is no longer I who did it, but the sin living in me that does it. (Romans 7:18–20)

As long as we live and breathe, we will possess the sinful nature that will never go away, which was why Christ came and died for us. Mosaic law wasn't enough because of the desires of the flesh, so God sent His Son to die, which gave us a chance to start over. We must acknowledge and embrace the fact that we possess sinful natures. What is sin?

> [The] Bible presents sin as an inner force, an inherent condition, a controlling power that lies at the core of our being. (Collins 1993, 97)

Part of self-knowledge and discovery, as mentioned in chapter 2, is understanding the significance our having a sinful nature through inheritance. Because we inherited and possess it, it holds us back or down. This means that our personality types are also affected by it. Therefore, we have no choice but to admit to it.

> We may as well admit to it. Every one of us from Adam's race has a share in putting Him on the cross! (Tozer 1976, 62)

What does all this mean? By acknowledging and embracing the fact that He came and died for us, we pave the way for God to take over our minds, bodies, and spirits again. Our personality types cannot effectively function or survive unless they are aligned with our spiritual types. When they collide, real life begins. We really don't have to take an assessment to acknowledge, accept, and come to terms with it. Yes, it is that simple.

Now that we have acknowledged and accepted this fact, what's next?

Acknowledgement and Acceptance, Part II

He is not here; He has risen, just as He said. Come and see the place where he lay. (Matthew 28:6)

But God demonstrates His own love for us in this: While we were still sinners, Christ died for us. (Romans 5:8)

For God so loved the world that He gave his one and only Son, that whoever believes in Him shall not perish but have eternal life. (John 3:16)

If you declare with your mouth, "Jesus is Lord," and believe in your heart that God raised Him from the dead, you will be saved.

For it is with your heart that you believe and are justified, and it is with your mouth that you profess your faith and are saved. (Romans 10:9–10)

The four verses above summed up everything you need to know. Just as the one act by Adam and Eve led to our sinful nature (Genesis 3), God also used one final act by letting His Son die on the cross to erase it for good. From everything I have presented to you, it is evident that God never stopped loving us and never stopped implementing effective ways to restore us.

Think back—there likely were many situations in which others gave us tangible gifts for Christmas, birthdays, and so on, but we chose to toss that aside or throw it away. Many times, we take for granted the gifts that someone gives us from the heart. We reject or send gifts back in so many ways, shapes, and forms. Sometimes, we don't even realize that we are doing so at that moment, but we recognize how essential that gift was when it becomes a memory.

Have you found yourself in such a situation, but it was too late? We may not take a lot of things seriously, so can you imagine how much we take for granted whatever we can't see seriously? I am no exception.

The death and Resurrection of Jesus Christ should never be taken lightly or be compared to any other gift. Christ's death and His Resurrection was the most significant event and eternal gift from God that no one should take for granted.

> I don't think there is anything harder on a preacher than knowing people in his congregation who need Jesus Christ, presenting the Gospel to them, and watching them neglect the possibility of salvation. (Jeremiah 1997, 20)

We have the mental capability to accept Jesus as our personal Savior. By doing so, we have nothing to lose and everything to gain, both physically and spiritually. Canadian theologian and author A. B. Simpson said it best:

> [Jesus's death] takes away the guilt of sin. It saves us from the wrath of God. It delivers us from the curse of the law. It also delivers us from our evil conscience. It delivers from the evil heart, which is the source of all sins in life. It frees us from the fear of death. It delivers us from Satan's power and kingdom. Beyond all else, it delivers us from eternal death. (2014, 3)

Earlier, I addressed the significance of merging our physical personal types and our spiritual types. The eternal spiritual aspects of our lives tremendously balance our physical types. Without it, life becomes more complicated or unbearable.

Remember that when it's time for you to pass and travel to the other side, your personality type dies with you; your spiritual aspect is eternal. God can help you save your personality type to succeed in life and your spiritual type after death. It is a win/win situation. Only *you* can do this for you.

We owe God a debt from the beginning of creation to this day. It is transcendent. We were made clean again. It is that simple. You might have experienced the following as a student: You walked into class on the first day, and the instructor tells you that your grade is an A+. All you have to do now is maintain it. Once you believe in your heart and profess with your mouth that Jesus died and was resurrected, you are saved.

> Jesus straightened up and asked her, "Woman, where are they? "Has no one condemned you?" "No one, sir," she said. "Then neither do I condemn you." Jesus declared. "Go now and leave your life of sin." (John 8:10–11)

When you have a few minutes, listen to the song "Forever (LIVE)" by Kari Jobe.

Acknowledgement and Acceptance, Part III

> After he said this, he was taken up before their very eyes, and a cloud hid him from their sight. They were looking intently up into the sky as he was going, when suddenly two men dressed in white stood beside them. "Men of Galilee," they said, "why do you stand here looking into the sky? This same Jesus, who has been taken from you into heaven, will come back in the same way you have seen him go into heaven." (Acts 1:9–11)

Some people struggle to grasp this part or to have confidence in it. I have spoken to many people who were on a shaky ground or skeptical about Jesus's imminent coming. Some have said, "I don't think that will happen during my lifetime. That passage was just meant to keep our focus on Him. Don't worry about that part." Others pointed out that the word *soon* was vague, and some said, "The day I'm on my deathbed will be His return for me."

Sadly, I was one of those people many years ago. There should be no debate. If we believe that our sinful nature from Adam and Eve triggered Jesus's coming and His death and that He is our personal Lord and Savior, then we should accept that His return is imminent. We should be on alert (Matthew 24:42–44).

While traveling to Helen, Georgia, I pondered Jesus's return. I recognized how much we tie God's hands by picking and choosing what we believe about Him and what we don't. Some Christians believe that God the Father, Son, and Holy Spirit exist to a limit. They also limit God's power, thereby eliminating some parts of God's nature, work, and power by claiming that Christ no longer does certain things, as He did while He was on earth. Certain things He did then do not apply today.

It feels like some of us created a perfect square box that we carry on our shoulders for all eyes to see, which communicates to others how little the Trinity is. Our God is omnipotent and omniscience. We should not put Him in a box or limit His nature. We should not pick and choose what, when, where, and how God fits our individual narratives. If we, the Christians, limit God's nature, existence, power, and might, what does that communicate to others who are struggling to believe or who don't believe at all? If we pick and choose who God is and is not, we should not be disappointed with those who do not believe or act the same way. Acknowledging and accepting Him requires full surrender. Therefore, if we acknowledge and accept that our sinful natures put Him on the cross and that He died and rose again, then we must acknowledge that He will return, and it's imminent. His imminent return cannot be diminished or minimized.

> The fact that the Old Testament prophets did not identify the Rapture by no means diminishes its importance. The New Testament makes up for the omission, giving us three central passages [John 14:1–3; 1 Corinthians 15:50–57; 1 Thessalonians 4:13–18] that record the details of this event. (Jeremiah 2016, 245)

The Bible described in Matthew 24 that the day and hour were unknown. Christ stated, "Two men will be in the field; one will be taken and the other left" (Matthew 24:40). No wonder I don't want to hang around other men anymore.

Listen to the song "My Deliverer" by Rich Mullins

The Case for Baptism of the Spirit and of Water

> Now there was a Pharisee, a man named Nicodemus who was a member of the Jewish ruling council. He came to Jesus at night and said, "Rabbi, we know that you are a teacher who has come from God. For no one could perform the signs you are doing if God were not with him." Jesus replied, "Very truly I tell you, no one can see the kingdom of God unless they are born again." "How can someone be born when they are old?" Nicodemus asked. "Surely they cannot enter a second time into their mother's womb to be born!" Jesus answered, "Very truly I tell you, no one can enter the kingdom of God unless they are born of water and the Spirit. Flesh gives birth to flesh, but the Spirit gives birth to spirit. You should not be surprised at my saying, 'You must be born again.' The wind blows wherever it pleases. You hear its sound, but you cannot tell where it comes from or where it is going. So, it is with everyone born of the Spirit." (John 3:1–8)

Jesus explained it very clearly. Once you accept Christ into your heart and proclaim Him as the Savior of the world, you immediately get baptized by the Holy Spirit.

> Apparently, he knew a great many in the audience because he would point to someone and also, "Brother, have you been baptized with the Spirit?" And the man would answer, "Yes, bless God." "Young man," he said, spotting me, "have you been baptized with the Holy Spirit?" "Yes, sir," I

replied. "When were you baptized with the Holy Spirit?" he asked. He had not questioned the others on this. "The moment I receive Jesus Christ as my savior," I replied. He looked at me with a puzzled expression, but before going to the next person he said," "That couldn't be." But it could. It was." (Graham 1988, 66)

You see, once you accept and proclaim Him, the Holy Spirit takes total control immediately. There is no waiting period. So many churches go back and forth with this topic, missing the point or losing the opportunity to focus on what really matters—that someone received Christ. I asked myself, "Didn't Christ die to abolish these man-made rules and regulations?" While water baptism is also essential, it is crucial to focus on acknowledging and celebrating the soul that Christ won for His glory at that very moment. Everything else will fall into place as the individual grows.

Throughout Christ's time on earth, He emphasized the Trinity (God in three persons: God the Father, God the Son, and God the Holy Spirit). "I and the Father are one" (John 10:30).

Christ also said,

> And I will ask the Father and He will give you another Counselor to be with you forever—the Spirit of truth. The world cannot accept him because it neither sees nor knows him. But you know him, for he lives with you and will be with you. (John 14:16–17)

Let me also cite the Old Testament in which God referenced "us" as plural when the earth was being created (Genesis 1:26). The point I am trying to make is that God the Father, Son, and Holy Spirit live in you. It's the duty and decision of the one born anew to take that step toward water baptism, not the church. There is nothing wrong with the church providing evidence of why water baptism is essential, but it should not be forced. Christ is the one doing the work, not us! Accepting Christ requires total surrender. No half-and-half business if we truly want the Trinity to live in us.

> The fact that we are passive in regeneration is also evident when the Scripture refers to it as being "born" or being "born again." We did not choose to be physically alive and we did not choose to be born—it is something that happened to us; similarly, these analogies in Scripture suggest that we are entirely passive to regeneration. (Grudem 1994, 699)

Song: "I Surrender" by Hillsong

God is completely moving into our lives. That is beyond a privilege. By the way, a privilege is a special right given to an individual or a group of individuals. To me, the word *privilege* is an understatement. In his book *Walking in the Spirit*, A. B. Simpson stated,

> Having led the soul to Christ, the Holy Spirit now becomes its personal, permanent, indwelling guest; bringing with Him the Manifested presence of the Father and the Son, leading into all truth, guiding in all the will of God, supplying all the needed grace, unfolding the life of Jesus Christ in the believer's daily life, and developing all the fruits of the Spirit in their full variety and complete maturity. (1889, 456)

Another book that comes to mind is *The Holy Spirit* (1978) by Billy Graham, in which he detailed who the Holy Spirit is and what it means to be filled with the Holy Spirit. Grab a copy and study it. There are many trusted Christian authors who will strengthen your understanding of the Holy Spirit, but the most important book to read is the Bible. Everyone possesses the fruits of the Spirit upon acceptance of Christ as one's personal Savior. The gifts of the Spirit, however, are geared more toward an individual's ministry.

Each of us is assigned with a unique spiritual power that we use to worship and draw others to Christ.

> Every believer receives these gifts at the moment of accepting Jesus Christ as personal savior. They are intended to be the main avenue through which a person ministers to others within the church as a whole (...) They are gifts that compel and inspire us to act in specific ways. (Stanley 2010, 3)

Sometimes, it's more than one, and it might take some time to recognize what you are or what they are. Understanding your personality type can play a role in understanding your gift of the Spirit. In fact, some individuals utilize their personality types as their ministry.

So what are the fruits of the Spirit and gifts of the Spirit? As indicated in Galatians 5:22–23, the fruit is love, joy, peace, forbearance, kindness, goodness, faithfulness, gentleness, and self-control. With regard to the gifts of the Spirit, 1 Corinthians 12:4–11 and Romans 12 state,

> There are different kinds of gifts, but the same Spirit distributes them. There are different kinds of service, but the same Lord. There are different kinds of working, but in all of them and in everyone it is the same God at work. Now to each one the manifestation of the Spirit is given for the common good. To one there is given through the Spirit a message of wisdom, to another a message of knowledge by means of the same Spirit, to another faith by the same Spirit, to another gifts of healing by that one Spirit, to another miraculous powers, to another prophecy, to another distinguishing between spirits, to another speaking in different kinds of tongues, and to still another the interpretation of tongues. All these are the work of one and the same Spirit, and he distributes them to each one, just as he determines.

Many spiritual assessment inventories are available at Christianbook.com—visit their site. Consult with your trusted Christian colleagues or leaders at your local church for recommendations and help.

From my perspective, two major points about the Holy Spirit is that He cannot be taken for granted and cannot be abused. He has feelings too (Ephesians 4:30). We take for granted, abuse, or grieve Him when we sin.

> When we disobey, God the Father is grieved, much as earthly father is grieved with his children's disobedience, and he disciplines us. (Grudem 1994, 505)

We possess a powerful tool—the brain—in our physical bodies that helps us make decisions. Can you imagine what can happen when our brains and the Holy Spirit collide and work together? It's beyond amazing or explanation. Wonders happen. It doesn't matter what your personality type is or your IQ, your location, your education, or your social-economic status. The Holy Spirit works the same way for everyone—one God, one Son, and one Spirit. There are so many functions of the Holy Spirit. It could not be measured in any way, shape, or form. In other words, His functions are limitless. It encompasses everything we can imagine. A few that stand out to me are as follows: He provides a bridge between God and me. He teaches me constantly and directs, reminds, and convicts me; He reveals to me and sets me apart for God alone.

More so, we should not fail to recognize that the fruits and gifts came from Him.

To turn the page, why is water baptism necessary? It is because Christ modeled it for us. He pointed out that it was proper for the fulfillment of all righteousness (Matthew 3:13–15).

> In water immersing, the believer physically enacts his/her death, burial to sin and resurrection to new life in Christ by being immersed in and raised up from the water. Water baptism can also be enacted through the pouring of water on the head of a believer in Christ, symbolizing repentances, cleansing of sin and outpouring of the Holy Spirit on a believer. (Gauthier 2022, 206)

The simple way to understand this is to follow Christ's footsteps or His actions while He was on earth. You will be secure and will never be disappointed or misled. Christ did not just come to die and resurrect. He also did other things, such as teaching, directing, and performing miracles, signs, wonders. He modeled how to live a pure life for us. In this case, there is nothing wrong in copying Christ and using the same behaviors He displayed or modeled for us. This is a privilege we should not let go to waste. Sometimes, some individuals need help with understanding the process of water baptism, even though the Holy Spirit was installed right after the individual accepted Christ as his or her personal Savior. One example occurred in Acts of the Apostles 8:26–40. After Philip explained the passage to the Ethiopian eunuch, he was baptized in the name of the Father, Son, and Holy Spirit.

Don't feel embarrassed. Read, but let someone you trust guide you through the process. Each church has its own protocol. After all is said and done, it leads to the same result. Another great example was presented to us in Acts 10:1–48. In this chapter, even though Cornelius and his family feared God, gave to others, and prayed constantly, they still needed to be saved through the death and Resurrection of Jesus Christ. Through the Holy Spirit, God linked him with Peter, who shared the Word of God with him and his family and then asked this question: "Can anyone keep these people from being baptized with water?" (Acts 10:47).

Many other examples may come to mind.

> The evidence, then, which I have sought to gather from the New Testament in general, and in particular from Peter's sermon in Acts 2 and Paul's teaching in 1 Corinthians 12:13, indicates that the "baptism" of the Spirit is identical with the "gift" of the Spirit, that it is one of the distinctive blessings of the new covenant and, because it is an initial blessing, is also a universal blessing for members of the covenant (Stott 2021, 57)

My True Eternal Identity

> You must begin with God, your Creator. You exist only because God wills that you exist. You were made by God and for God—and until you understand that, life will never make sense. It is only in God that we discover our origin, our identity, our meaning, our purpose, our significance, and our destiny. Every other path leads to a dead end. (Warren 2002, 18)

About three years ago, I had coffee with a good friend whom I hadn't seen in many years. We discussed different topics as we enjoyed the waves of the beach. She informed me that she had taken an online test that helped her identify who her ancestors were. I found it interesting and asked a couple of follow-up questions. She seemed very excited about her lineage, and I congratulated her for finding that out. She immediately texted me the link and encouraged me to take the test.

"That's nice of you," I said, "but I already know my lineage. Would you like to know?"

She said yes, with a very curious expression on her face.

I told her I was from Africa, the motherland.

She burst out laughing and said, "Duh! I knew that."

I laughed with her and added that I was also a Christian.

She paused for a few seconds and asked, "What does Christianity have to do with the discussion?"

I responded, "It has to do with every fiber of my being."

I had wholeheartedly listened to her story and ideas and that she wanted me to try the test. I felt like I wanted to share my story and ideas, and I wanted her to try mine. It was a great opportunity for me to explain that there was no other way for anyone to find his or her true identity or origin (Genesis 1:27; Psalm 82:6; Galatians 4:7) and no other way anyone can be saved, other than through Christ (Ephesians 2:8–10).

A lot of people are suffering and searching for answers, but they are going along the wrong routes to find it.

> Come to me, all you who are weary and burdened, and I will give you rest. Take my yoke upon you and learn from me, for I am gentle and humble in heart, and you will find rest for your souls. For my yoke is easy and my burden is light. (Matthew 11:28–30)

This promise is genuine and within your reach. We have such scattered brains that we do not even realize it. It's like craving a particular product, going to the store to buy it, and then, when you get home, realizing you already have it. Sometimes we get so obsessed about finding the truth about ourselves or our identities that others take advantage of us by ripping us off. We already have access to all the answers to the questions we are seeking.

Your origin, worth, purpose, fate, and destiny are all found in one book—the Bible. I have had my share of doubts in the past and present, and I'm sure I'll have some doubts lingering in the future. One thing I know for sure, however, without a doubt, is that I am how I am and where I am because that's how and where God wants me to be. It took me some time to understand this. Sometimes I wonder about myself, but I do my best to trust God every day and not rely on my own interpretations or understanding (Proverbs 3:5–6). We do not have to be rocket scientists to comprehend that God created us in His image and died for us in order to for us to regain our pure identity. The bottom line: if you don't have a Bible, get one. Study, believe, accept, and apply it, and never look back.

Listen to the song "Jump" by Nonah.

The Bible

His book, the Bible, describes His plan of Salvation. The purpose of the Bible is to proclaim God's plan and passion to save His children (...) The Bible is the treasure map that leads to God's highest treasure—eternal life. (Lucado 2018, vi)

So, why get a Bible? Why study, believe, accept, and apply the Bible in your life? You should implement those steps because the Word of God (Bible) is His breath.

All Scripture is God-breathed and is useful for teaching, rebuking, correcting and training in righteousness, so that the servant of God may be thoroughly equipped for every good work. (2 Timothy 3:16–17)

I realized two major things, among many others, about my physical health. If I don't eat an apple a day or take at least a mile walk, I do not operate well the next day. Note that this is just about my *physical* health and well-being. With regard to my spiritual health, if I don't read the Bible each day, I am psychologically lost or drained.

If we do as much as we can to nurture our physical bodies, why wouldn't we do the same to nurture our spirits?

Heaven is now silent; God the Creator has spoken, and the Bible is His written word. God made himself known on the stage of history by prophecy, by providence, by miracle, and supremely in His Son, Jesus Christ; and Scripture witnesses to that. God disclosed His will for the living of our lives, and the Bible proclaims His law. (Packer 1995, 43)

I am not big about arguing back and forth with anyone about the Word of God. We, the people, love to taste something before we make decisions for ourselves. I taste wine, food, things, places, and so on. Why not "taste" the Bible to make your own decision?

The first step in understanding the Bible is asking God to help you (...) Before reading the Bible, pray and invite God to speak to you. Don't go to Scripture looking for your idea, but go searching for His. (Lucado 2018, vi)

The Bible is very sophisticated and can be hard to comprehend at times. So many things in it may cause individuals to wonder why God allowed certain things to happen. Reading it and comprehending it are two different things. Don't worry—you can get help. Before Christ's death, He made many promises to us. One of those promises was about sending us a counselor, the Holy Spirit.

But the Advocate, the Holy Spirit, whom the Father will send in my name, will teach you all things and will remind you of everything I have said to you. (John 14:26)

But when he, the Spirit of truth, comes, he will guide you into all the truth. He will not speak on his own; he will speak only what he hears, and he will tell you what is yet to come. (John 16:13)

You need not worry. You are covered. The Holy Spirit, the Comforter, settled in you when you accepted Christ. He's eagerly waiting to share you with the Father and the Son.

Personally speaking, I have been through a lot in my life. Many friends and family suffered through those challenges with me. During those trials, it was easy to doubt.

It's very easy to toss the Bible aside and stop listening to the Comforter. That's human nature, but you must keep reading and nourishing yourself with the Word of God. During those times, I am reminded that what is happening is meant to be happening at that particular moment. Also, the Counselor is there with me to support, process, and understand what's going on and how to combat it.

There was always a reason something was happening at that very moment, even though I did not comprehend it. In fact, sometimes the reason could be that I lost focus and stopped depending on Him. Maybe my ego got in the way. I just have to trust God without a shadow of doubt. Many times, I was directed to read a particular passage. Even though I'd read it previously, I was directed to read it again and again until I comprehended what I was being told to read. I am very stubborn and weak—who isn't, right?—but I do my best each time to listen and obey.

> It is better to take refuge in the Lord than to trust humans. It is better to take refuge in the Lord than trust in princes. (Psalm 118:8–9)

There were times when I threw temper tantrums and argued back and forth with the Spirit because something wasn't making any sense to me. There were times when I had conversations with Him.

He always listens and is very patient. He redirects and never misleads me.

> There have been times I've been distracted and times when I felt like I was being destroyed, times when I was discouraged and disappointed and even felt defeated. But here's what I've learned: When those things start happening, it's because you've lost your focus. When I start feeling those emotions, I have to shut down and get away some place with my Bible, my notebook, and my journal. I have to back away from all the pressure and say, "Lord, I am starting to feel things I shouldn't feel if I stay focused. Now help me to get focused again." (Jeremiah 2020, 63)

Stay connected with your Bible with the assistance of the Holy Spirit; study through thick and thin. Also, there are other ways to get the help you need to understand what God is communicating with you through his Word. I said earlier that we shouldn't feel embarrassed to seek help from trusted lay ministers at church. When you read a passage in the Bible that was a bit difficult to comprehend, there always will be someone you can trust at your local church—or even from other churches—who is gifted and ready to spend time with you. Some individuals end up being accountable to each other for growth purposes. Never be ashamed to speak up and ask questions. Each of us needs help with comprehending God's view when we are stuck. We have the right to seek, ask, and knock. Also, we deserve to get the right answers.

> Ask and it will be given to you; seek and you will find; knock and the door will be opened to you. For everyone who asks receives; the one who seeks finds; and to the one who knocks, the door will be opened. (Matthew 7:7–8)

Meeting Together

> And let us consider how we may spur one another on toward love and good deeds, not giving up meeting together, as some are in the habit of doing, but encouraging one another—and all the more as you see the Day approaching. (Hebrews 10:24–25)

Life is very busy. We are always on the go. We make sure others are nurtured, happy, strong, healthy, and so on. We love to be needed and to be where we are needed. I've mentioned that we are good at telling others what to do. We also spend time doing exercise, eating healthfully, losing weight, and having a desire to live longer and avoid major illness. We shouldn't forget to nurture the Holy Spirit in us. Realistically speaking, if we can make time for everyone and everything else underneath the sun, we can make time for a small group or fellowship with others for one to two hours a week. A *small group* refers to a gathering of a few Christians who discuss and examine the Bible. Small groups strengthen and edify their members. We need those interactions with others to reenergize, to understand how to use our swords (the Bible), and to keep our swords sharpened and cleaned. It is also where great, sad, or uncomfortable topics are discussed for clarity.

> As iron sharpens iron, so one person sharpens another. (Proverbs 27:17)

Do you want to be relevant in truth, in Spirit, in your life, in everything and everyone around you? A small group is the answer. We need as much support as possible on our spiritual journeys.

> For where two or three gather in my name, there am I with them. (Matthew 18:20; Acts 2:42–47; 17:11–12; Galatians 6:2; Ephesians 4:15–16; 1 Thessalonians 5:11; Hebrews 10:24–25; James 5:16)

We cannot effectively combat life's challenging circumstances alone to talk of spiritual warfare. Spiritual warfare is a biblical concept used by Christians to describe a fight against spiritual evil forces (Ephesians 6:10–20).

I worked with two important people, Steve Joyce and Dave Bartholdson, in church, and I respect them to this day. When my life's boat tipped over, I disconnected from everyone, but these two men kept in touch and considered me their brother. We need more people like them. It is crucial to get connected with a small group. You will get the support and spiritual nutrients you deserve, regardless of your circumstances. During a time of trouble, need, or life's turbulence, there are children of God who are gifted in that area to provide you with the extra shield you need at that moment. Remember that not everyone in the church possesses that gift. Those who are gifted in that particular area will know what to do.

I am very bad at taking care of plants, both outdoors and indoors. I get very excited when I buy them, but they do not last long, even though I water them and nurture them. While I was fixing up my front landscape, a friend suggested the type of potting soil to use. I bought exactly what she recommended. I bought two golden pothos plants. Since I had some leftover outdoor potting soil, I thought, *Why waste the money on indoor potting soil? They're all soil.* Three weeks later, I started seeing a lot of fungus gnats everywhere in the house. My house is very clean, and I wasn't sure where they originated. That same day, I moved the plant to water it, and there they were. I frantically opened my front door and took those plants outside. Lesson learned! There were many gnats on both plants.

I received many great suggestions for effectively caring for plants, but the best one was a suggestion to start speaking to them. I looked at her and said, "My good friend, I do not want to be Baker Acted." (The Baker Act, also known as the Florida Mental Health Act, was established by the state of Florida in 1972 to allow for the creation of more mental health programs geared toward alleviating the occurrence, duration, and severity of psychological and behavioral disorders, as a means to prevent severe harm to self or others. While I used the Baker Act in that context, it was not used as a means to degrade the Baker Act programs in any way.)

You can't trust me when it comes to gardening, but we do have Someone who is great at it. God is the Gardener, Christ is the Vine, and we are the branches (John 15:1–17). We bear fruits through examining the Bible every day and engaging in small groups.

> He became the true Vine, that we might be true branches. Both in regard to Christ and ourselves the words teach us the two lessons of absolute dependence and perfect confidence. (Murray 2011, 4)

Prayer of a Broken and Contrite Heart

Pray continually. (1 Thessalonians 5:17)

Several passages in both in the Old and New Testaments emphasize the importance and benefits of praying. To name a few, read Genesis 18; 2 Kings 6; 2 Kings 19; Daniel 9; Matthew 26:36–45; Mark 11:22–25; Philippians 4:6; James 5:13–19; and 1 John 5:14. What about King David, who was always on the run for various reasons and prayed constantly? Another passage that stands out for me is Genesis 32:22–32, in which Jacob wrestled God for His blessings. Even though God wrenched his hip out of socket, Jacob held on and said, "I will not let you go until you bless me" (Genesis 32:26). Jacob was persistent, determined, and focused, and he knew exactly what he was asking for—God's blessings.

As I played out this event in my head, I could picture Jacob saying the same thing over and over again—"Bless me." Then I wondered what it really means to be blessed by God. It is limitless and can come in many ways, shapes, and forms. But Jacob did not care what kind of blessing he was getting. He simply wanted to be blessed. It was an opportunity for him, and he had no intention of letting go until he was blessed. That is the heart of prayer that God seeks.

In this day and age, I have noticed that the significance of prayer has diminished. We use the word *prayer* loosely, and it seems that it does not have a value, but it does. In Matthew 6:5–14, Christ gave us prayer instructions and also modeled it for us.

> His instructions were not only direct, but extensive and profound. He did not teach His disciples how to preach but He certainly guided them as to how they should pray and approach the mercy seat. (Lockyer 1999, 139)

There were many times He separated from His disciples to pray alone. In this passage, He demonstrated how to pray in the Spirit, not in the flesh. Since the Holy Spirit is in us, then our prayers should be in the Spirit, not in a worldly way. Prayers we bring up that focus on the desires of our flesh are not profitable for the Spirit.

How do you pray? What does your prayer life look like? When was the last time you went into your room and closed the door to pray? When was the last time you knelt down to pray? Do you constantly pray without ceasing? Do you praise and worship God in your prayer? Do you ask for His will to be done (no strings attached)? Do you pray for here and now (to guide and help you survive today)? Do you pray to forgive others who have wronged you, as He forgave you? How about safeguarding you from evil? When you promise to pray for someone, do you really pray for them? Sometimes, my prayers are not what they need to be or are intended to be. It's more about "give me, give me, give me."

> God wants us to pray and He wants to answer our prayers, but He makes our use of prayer as a privilege to commingle with His use of prayer as a discipline. To receive answers to prayer we must meet God's terms. If we neglect His commandments our petitions will not be honored. He will alter situations only at the request of obedient and humble souls. (Tozer 2016, 167)

A lot of things we ask for in prayers are considered acts or things that would glorify Him. When we ask, we should not go overboard with our requests. To God, all things are possible, but I have asked for many things that, although possible to God, were inappropriate for me. In my mind at that particular juncture, I thought it was perfect for me. Why? Because I wanted it right then and there, without envisioning the negative impacts the request could have in the future.

God heard me, but He also sees the future and would not want me to be harmed. Remember the saying, "Be careful what you wish for"? God sometimes grants our wishes, only for us to turn around and blame Him for granting those requests. When you pray, go after God's heart first. Keep it simple. Constantly pray for His blessings and for His will. When we seek His kingdom and His righteousness first, everything else will fall into place. Read Matthew 6:25–34. It's all about how, where, when, and what we want.

My prayers were all about my agenda, not God's. There were a handful of things that, when I thought of them, bothered me or broke me down. But God kept telling me to stay focused and wait for Him (Psalm 27:14).

The following is one of those verses that God kept bringing up and repeating to me. I learned to ask just for His blessings and will. You should do the same.

> The sacrifices of God are a broken spirit; a broken and contrite heart, O God, You will not despise. (Psalm 51:17)

There is absolutely nothing wrong with praying for specific things. We are privileged to ask for whatever we need from Him. Always remember this part—may His will be done—in each circumstance. Trust that He will make the best decision for you. If you don't know what to pray for or where to start because you are broken due to your circumstances, praise Him.

I would like you to listen to the songs "I Will Sing" and "Our Father" by Don Moen. God hears you! Those songs uplift me every time I feel broken down.

> And my God will meet all your needs according to the riches of his glory in Christ Jesus (Philippians 4:19)

We Have Unique Lives to Live

> Live such good lives among the pagans that, though they accuse you of doing wrong, they may see your good deeds and glorify God on the day he visits us. (1 Peter 2:12)

Our behaviors and actions are testimonies to others from the time we wake up to the time we go to bed. Witnessing happens every second of the day. It doesn't necessarily mean standing at the pulpit all the time. The morals and values we display to others matter. One major way to fulfill the law is to love your neighbor as yourself (Galatians 5:14). The best character witness for you is love. Love is lacking severely in the world today. Just look around you. It is lacking, suppressed, limited, and very scarce. It is running excessively low in our world today. The world craves love. Love is the most important type of vitamin that the majority of people are lacking. We possess it, and this is our opportunity to share.

> How do God's people live in a godless society? Blend in and assimilate? No, this is the time to stand out and assist. We were made for this moment. (Lucado 2021, 28)

God is love. He has shown what it looks like and has shared it with us. If that is the case, then we are love as well.

> My command is this: Love each other as I have loved you. Greater love has no one than this: to lay down one's life for one's friends. (John 15:12–13)

Some of us wonder where or how to expand the kingdom of God. Why not start with love? Just take a look in a mirror. All you will see is love. It is overflowing and must be shared with others. If you can focus on love alone, you will become the kind of love that talks, walks, touches, feels, and sees. The love given to us is limitless. Therefore, the love we show others should be limitless.

> Love should be your first priority, primary objective, and greatest ambition. Love is not a good part of your life; it's the most important part. (Warren 2002, 124)

If you claim you love and worship God in truth and in Spirit, then make time to love others—not just people with whom you attend church services but the world's audience, who are watching every move you make. Don't love for self-gratification, but love because it's a command from Christ. An individual can witness to others through his or her behavior and actions. When you love others just as God loves you, you leave the door open to share your experiences about God. If love is put on the back burner, that means God's agenda is also put on the back burner. As a result, your green light will be very blurry. You will get confused on whether you should forge ahead or not. In fact, it will be difficult for others to take you seriously, and they will not show any interest in finding out more about you and what you stand for. Make a note of that.

> This is how we know what love is: Jesus Christ laid down his life for us. And we ought to lay down our lives for our brothers and sisters. If anyone has material possessions and sees a brother or sister in need but has no pity on them, how can the love of God be in that person? Dear children, let us not love with words or speech but with actions and in truth (1 John 3:16–18)

Each of us possesses the fruits of the Spirit, but we also possess one or more gifts that are geared toward building and expanding God's kingdom. It's time to put those gifts assigned to you to work through your local church or wherever God desires you to be. They were not given to you to be put on your living room shelf. They are not trophies because trophies are put on a display for everyone to see and so you can toot your horn. Your gifts are not tools to put away to prevent anyone from using them. Also, they are not collectable. They are meant to be used toward whatever ministry God calls you to do through your church and outside your church.

From my perspective, all the gifts identified in 1 Corinthians 12 are functional to this day. In that chapter, Paul indicated the significance of each gift and expressed that none of the gifts was better than the other. For some reason, some individuals are not satisfied with the gifts given to them. As a result, they abandon what they should be doing and engage in areas God did not ordain. This causes a lot of confusion, strife, and chaos. If each of us stays in our own lanes, there will be order in the church and outside the church.

> For God is not a God of disorder but of peace—as in all the congregations of the Lord's people. (1 Corinthians 14:33)

There have been behind-the-scenes quarrels among the church or church leaders as to which spiritual gifts are applicable versus those which are not applicable. In fact, many have left their churches because they do not agree with their church's stance on this matter. The more the debate goes on in the church, the more we humans tie God's hands. It's impossible for someone to identify as a Christian while picking or choosing gifts that are applicable or no longer applicable.

> Do not add to what I command you and do not subtract from it, but keep the commands of the Lord your God that I give you. (Deuteronomy 4:2)

> I warn everyone who hears the words of the prophecy of this scroll: If anyone adds anything to them, God will add to that person the plagues described in this scroll. And if anyone takes words away from this scroll of prophecy, God will take away from that person any share in the tree of life and in the Holy City, which are described in this scroll. (Revelation 22:18–19)

That is a firm and clear warning! If we believe that God is the breath of God, then we should humbly not interfere in whatever God's doing or with the type of gift He uses to win souls for Himself. We should encourage or advocate for whichever gift God uses to win souls for Himself.

Total surrender to God is very difficult because of our human nature, but it's doable if we stay focused on what really matters—and that is complying with God's instructions (Bible). Trust and obey them. Our human personality types are skewed, but our spiritual types make us whole again. It's impossible for us to survive without this pathway. We can huff and puff all we want, but we need God in our lives. Remember that spirituality (through Christ) is like the chassis of a car. A chassis is the frame of every car and can be compared to the bones in our bodies. Without the chassis (our bones), we might as well be considered dead.

I am not perfect, and no one is, but the more we strive to be whole, the more God will use us without limits. We will be ready to do exactly what Matthew 28:19–20 tells us:

> Therefore go and make disciples of all nations, baptizing them in the name of the Father and of the Son and of the Holy Spirit, and teaching them to obey everything I have commanded you. And surely I am with you always, to the very end of the age.

When fate knocks at your door, you will open that door with boldness and confidence. When it lashes out at you from different angles, regardless of how bad the circumstance is, God will always be there with you. He will provide you with peace and comfort. He will never leave you alone, even when everyone else abandons you. Remember Job? He lost everything but stayed connected with God. Referring to Matthew 14:22–32, Max Lucado (2020) states,

> We never expect to see Him in a storm. But it is in storms that He does His finest work, for it is in the storms that He has our keenest attention. (42)

Now you are ready to start the engine with your key, self-will or free will.

"Whole Heart" by Hillsong Worship

CHAPTER 5

FREE WILL: GOD'S ORDAINED GIFT TO HUMANKIND

"Resurrection Power" by Chris Tomlin

Free Will Came with Instructions

> Now all has been heard; here is the conclusion of the matter: Fear God and keep his commandments, for this is the duty of all mankind. For God will bring every deed into judgment, including every hidden thing, whether it is good or evil (Ecclesiastes 12:13–14)

Free will is defined as a person's ability to act on anything without restrictions whatsoever. Throughout history, free will has been applied for good deeds, which is what God intended. Many, however, have abused this gift given by God. Instead of using it for good, some use it for evil against others, as evidenced by controlling, punishing, suppressing, deceiving, and oppressing. A lot of people have different views about free will, and it's OK to have differences of opinions. In his book *What about Free Will?*, Scott Christensen (2016) states, "In this regard, it is better to speak of people being free rather than the will being free—to speak of free agents, not free wills" (136).

I agree wholeheartedly with this view that Christ's blood will set us free. I would just add that God bestowed on us this amazing gift, free will, to worship Him in truth and spirit. It is beyond incredible for God to say to us,

> I said, "You are 'gods,'; you are all sons of the Most High." (Psalm 82:6)

Also, don't forget that He gave us the ability to reproduce, multiply, or subdue. This is beyond magnificent, and the fact the animals and plants He created can also reproduce in order to sustain our lives and live comfortably is what God's love is all about. He gave us so much power and inheritance. This is what is meant in Genesis 1:26—"He created us in His image."

The sad news, however, is that some people use their God-given abilities against God's ordained purposes for it. Everything we purchase comes with instructions of some sort. When we are born, we also come with instructions. When God created Adam and Eve, they came with instructions also. Right after God created Adam, He gave Adam instructions on how he must live his life.

> The Lord God took the man and put him in the Garden of Eden to work it and take care of it. And the Lord God commanded the man, "You are free to eat from any tree in the garden; but you must not eat from the tree of the knowledge of good and evil, for when you eat from it you will certainly die." (Genesis 2:15–17)

We all came with the same reliable instructions.

> If one discards the Bible as unreliable historically, then he or she must discard all the literature on antiquity. (McDowell and McDowell 2009, 87)

No one is excluded in this matter. Everything you do with the knowledge and power given to you matters a great deal. What are the instructions we came with? The answer is the one and only Bible. No one should contest this. Your true fate and destiny are to follow God's commandments.

In chapter 1, I presented the reality of life as it is. Chapter 2 focused on the pursuit of self-knowledge and discovery. Chapter 3 discussed the spiritual type and pathway, and I compared the spiritual type and pathway as the chassis of a car. In order for you to handle life or your fate, personality type, and spiritual path effectively, the Word of God must be engraved in you.

> Fix these words of mine in your hearts and minds; tie them as symbols on your hands and bind them on your foreheads. (Deuteronomy 11:18)

You cannot nurture your personality and spiritual type without knowledge and implementation of God's Word (the Bible). Just as we eat healthy food to stay healthy physically, we do the same by nourishing our spiritual health through the Bible. In his book, *Even in Our Darkness*, Jack Deere (2018) states, "We live from one crisis to the next" (12). Welcome to being human! The challenges or crises we face each time are not faced alone. God is always there with us and speaks to us through them. It's impossible, however, to hear Him in the mix of chaos or noises at those times unless you are linked with Him through His Word (the Bible).

I was just thinking about what the light actually means to me. We need lights in the day and the night. Has your electricity ever gone off at night, and you could not find where you left your flashlights, lantern, or even your phone? You were completely left in the dark. Remember how anxious and concerned you felt? Just compare that to not knowing or understanding God when you face a crisis. You are completely lost and left by yourself in the middle of nowhere. This is how Psalm 119:105 describes the Word of God: "Your word is a lamp for my feet, a light on my path." If an individual is troubled, panics, is in shock, or gets shaken up by the fact that the electricity goes out for whatever reason, imagine how that same individual will feel if he or she doesn't know his Creator when facing a crisis.

Our man-made technologies will always fade or disappoint us, but the light unto your feet and path (Word of God) will never fade, disappoint, or leave you out to dry. Yes, you have free will that comes with instructions that should never be taken for granted. I have never seen anyone who chose to walk in the dark without some sort of light. A lot of things can happen while you are in the dark simply because you cannot see. I am referring to man-made electricity. Many bad things can happen, such as tripping and falling or a simple but fatal accident. Someone close to me had a medical emergency; she hit her head and never woke up from it.

Many things can happen when we walk around without man-made electricity. When we stumble, which words come out of our mouths? "Jesus Christ" or "Oh my God," right? During emergencies, we never scream, "Oh Satan, oh devil, oh darkness!" We always scream or look to connect with God in emergencies. Do you have friends who never say hello or check up on you, but they call on you when they're in need? I know exactly how you feel about that. If you feel as I do and ignore those calls, imagine how God feels. The difference between us and God, though, is that He always comes to our rescue.

> Nevertheless, there are many who choose not to explore the deeper questions of where and who God is. Our life experiences can encourage or discourage a need or desire to seek God. Ironically, I have observed that it is pain rather than joy that is most likely to compel someone toward a journey into faith. Perhaps, this is because pain alerts us to a condition we don't have any power to fix. (Short 2014, 54)

Another example is how much emphasis we put on our cell phones. Possessing a cell phone is the best thing life can offer; some people will mock you for not having one. We cannot do without it. The good, bad, and ugly have happened through our cell phones. Think of when phone calls or text messages brought good news or bad and ugly news and how you reacted toward each type of news. When we are without our phones, it seems like the end of the world. We do not want to miss a tiny fraction of anything. We use them all the time to keep in touch with everyone—from our loved ones to those we don't know well. Most of us don't even turn off our phones at bedtime. In most cases, we carry extra battery chargers to ensure we stay connected.

Some people will find you contemptable for not answering their calls, even though you have more important things to attend to or even may have a crisis. Some consider others as outcasts for not having the same type of phone they have. They pressure the so-called outcasts to get the same type of phone in order to join the club and feel better about himself or herself, even though the person does not have the resources to afford it. Cell phone providers are also considered contemptible when there is no network available. Some people turn into monsters over their cell phones. Cell phones keep everyone connected even more than they should. They are perishable, but the Bible is not.

The Word of God (the Bible) keeps us connected with God. We spend an excessive amount of time on our cell phones every day, yet we find it difficult or impossible to spend fifteen minutes meditating on God. We have so many different apps on our phones, but ask an average person if he or she has a Bible app on his or her phone. By the way, just having a Bible application on our phones is not enough. We actually have to open it and study it.

Many of us have prayed for safe travel behind the wheel, and we blame God when we get into a car accident. "God, how could you let this happen?" Other examples might have crossed your mind as well. We put so much value on what we can see and hold. We should reverse it, as the apostle Paul said, "So we fix our eyes not on what is seen, but on what is unseen, since what is seen is temporary, but what is unseen is eternal" (2 Corinthians 4:18).

Staying connected with your Creator will save you from a lot of grief. It opens your mind and expands your horizons beyond what your eyes can see.

There was a period in my life when my primary physician advised me not to eat certain food, especially food that contains carbs, due to my diabetes. At one of the doctor's visits, she advised me to eat half a bagel instead of a full one. So I decided to eat half a bagel—with a full glazed or jelly doughnut with it. Indirectly, that doughnut made up for the half of the bagel I could not have. For more than a year, I noticed that my blood sugar would shoot up in the morning and crash by midafternoon until night, and I could not function. It seriously made me sick. I could not put my finger on it, so I mentioned it to my doctor's nurse, and she faxed a referral for blood and urine work.

Each morning, I ate the same food, and each afternoon, I had the same result. The result never changed—until I realized the source of the problem. It was me. It was my own doing because I ignored my doctor's instructions. While I was frustrated and expected her to fix it, she could not fix something that I created myself. I was the one who needed to recognize the dilemma and resolve it. So I changed my diet by decreasing the amount I consumed tremendously, and guess what? The problem was corrected.

Have you ever craved something you were not supposed to eat but ate it anyway, against doctor's orders? Did you pray to God that He would prevent you from getting sick after you ate the food that was forbidden for you? After eating it, did you get sick and then blame God for not preventing your getting sick? I think you get my point now. The Word of God is our manual, our map, and our one and only instruction book that we must read, meditate on, and follow every day. We must follow those guidelines. Each time we don't, the end result is always against our wishes. In it, it explains how to live and what to do and not do. With our human nature, we have a habit of ignoring God's clear and simple wishes, just because we have the free will to do so. Then, we can't handle the end results, and we blame God for letting it happen.

> This day I call the heavens and the earth as witnesses against you that I have set before you life and death, blessings and curses. Now choose life, so that you and your children may live and that you may love the Lord your God, listen to his voice, and hold fast to him. For the Lord is your life, and he will give you many years in the land he swore to give to your fathers, Abraham, Isaac and Jacob. (Deuteronomy 30:19–20)

You may be causing a lot of havoc in your life. If you follow your instruction book, the Bible, it will prevent you from walking down a route that is very dangerous or unhealthy for you.

Utilizing Your Free Will Properly

> For you were called to freedom, brothers. Only do not use your freedom as an opportunity for the flesh, but through love serve one another. (Galatians 5:13)

It is impossible to utilize your free will without God's grace. You cannot withstand the forces of fate and can't find your destiny if you don't follow the one and only instruction manual, the Bible.

> Therefore everyone who hears these words of mine and puts them into practice is like a wise man who built his house on the rock. The rain came down, the streams rose, and the winds blew and beat against that house; yet it did not fall, because it had its foundation on the rock. But everyone who hears these words of mine and does not put them into practice is like a foolish man who built his house on sand. The rain came down, the streams rose, and the winds blew and beat against that house, and it fell with a great crash. (Matthew 7:24–27)

Not being in tune with the Bible is like a car's tires being out of alignment. You would know. When you can identify who you are personally and your spiritual type, you will love and appreciate who you are and continue your life's journey through this instructional manual, the Bible.

September 2022 exposed a lot of things I suppressed, which broke me down. I felt like I was massively attacked with grief. I decided to leave Florida for a brief getaway in Helen, Georgia. While I was there, I read, meditated, and cried a lot. While I was there, I received a text from my ex-mother-in-law to remind me about a birthday of someone close to me. I had forgotten about it; in fact, I'd suppressed it.

As I was praying, I asked God to take the pain away and made a lot of requests, which were. extremely important to me—one, in particular—and God knew that. He never took any of my requests for granted, but the feedback I received, per the still small voice, was that some of those requests were not crises. They were what I wanted and not what I needed. My mind redirected me back to 1991, when I first stepped foot in the United States. I was flooded with three different flashbacks—first, how God guided and blessed me and never forsook me, as well as who and what He made me to be this very day. Second, there were flashbacks about the things I asked for that He did not grant, and I realized that could have been disastrous if He had granted those requests. Third, there were flashbacks of prayers He answered that I regretted asking for, and that taught me many lessons. I sure got it. Then I thought I should make a last-ditch effort and made one unprecedented request, which I thought could be a deal-breaker, as related to that one important request I made.

"Our lifespan was shortened due to Adam and Eve's sin, and they lived to be more than nine hundred years old anyways. Now that Christ has died and has taken away all our sins, could we go back to living more than nine hundred years?" I got no response to that request, but I could sense God laughing.

"Do It Again" by Elevation Worship

Four passages were presented to me:

> "For my thoughts are not your thoughts, neither are your ways my ways," declares the Lord. "As the heavens are higher than the earth, so are my ways higher than your ways and my thoughts than your thoughts." (Isaiah 55:8–9)

> When he saw Peter and John about to enter, he asked them for money. Peter looked straight at him, as did John. Then Peter said, "Look at us!" So the man gave them his attention, expecting to get something from them. Then Peter said, "Silver or gold I do not have, but what I do have I give you. In the name of Jesus Christ of Nazareth, walk." Taking him by the right hand, he helped him up, and instantly the man's feet and ankles became strong. He jumped to his feet and began to walk. Then he went with them into the temple courts, walking and jumping, and praising God. (Acts 3:3–8)

This next one is my favorite verse. Isn't it interesting how God uses passages we love to speak to us?

Wait for the Lord; be strong and take heart and wait for the Lord. (Psalm 27:14)

Therefore I tell you, do not worry about your life, what you will eat or drink; or about your body, what you will wear. Isn't life more than food, and the body more than clothes? Look at the birds of the air; they do not sow or reap or store away in barns, and yet your heavenly Father feeds them. Are you not much more valuable than they? Can any one of you by worrying add a single hour to your life? And why do you worry about clothes? See how the flowers of the field grow. They do not labor or spin. Yet I tell you that not even Solomon in all his splendor was dressed like one of these. If that is how God clothes the grass of the field, which is here today and tomorrow is thrown into the fire, will he not much more clothe you—you of little faith? So do not worry, saying, 'What shall we eat?' or 'What shall we drink?' or 'What shall we wear?' For the pagans run after all these things, and your heavenly Father knows that you need them. But seek first his kingdom and his righteousness, and all these things will be given to you as well. Therefore, do not worry about tomorrow, for tomorrow will worry about itself. Each day has enough trouble of its own. (Matthew 6:25–34)

God controls the narratives, not us. All we have to do is listen, obey, and live like Him and for Him alone. I immediately had to change my thoughts and prayers. I asked for Him to keep blessing me and that His will only would be done. I encourage you to read 1 Kings 3 in reference to Solomon's prayer for wisdom.

On September 13, 2022, I met with Steve Joyce and Jim and shared some of my experiences. They listened and encouraged me. Jim Gerald said that I was blessed and that I should just be still and know He's God. Their encouragement echoed back to some of what I heard.

Song: "Be Still and Know" by Don Moen

We utilize our free will for God's glory alone. In order to utilize your free will effectively and to minimize the desires or opportunities of the flesh, trust and obey God. He will guide your path. Everyone is an instrument for Him alone. When we seek His desires, His wishes, and His face, He goes beyond measure to bless us. When we face challenges or fate knocks on our doors, we can withstand whatever comes against us. Also, we will be able to discern whether whatever is happening is a test, an attack from the devil, or something that resulted from our stepping off the track. We just have a decision to make: to surrender fully to Him or not.

Now fear the Lord and serve him with all faithfulness. Throw away the gods your ancestors worshiped beyond the Euphrates River and in Egypt, and serve the Lord. But if serving the Lord seems undesirable to you, then choose for yourselves this day whom you will serve, whether the gods your ancestors served beyond the Euphrates, or the gods of the Amorites, in whose land you are living. But as for me and my household, we will serve the Lord. (Joshua 24:14–15)

For God to create us in His own image and then give us the ability to choose is beyond amazing. Choose to live your life in Christ, and refuse every offer the devil makes to you. Those offers from the devil only lead to misery in life and eternal death.

To this day, Satan attempts to lie to us to get us to accept him as God's replacement and as the center of their religious institution and personal lives. (Mora 2022, 101)

Do not entertain Satan's offers, but stay focused on God. Don't let Satan drag you down into the abyss with him. He's been defeated over and over again, and he will stay defeated forever! Take a second to think about this—if our sins triggered Jesus's coming, and He was mercilessly and brutally crucified on the cross, doesn't that tell you how much He values us? He not only values and loves us, but He also gave us the ability to choose and live freely. Why not choose Him and utilize your free will in ways that will honor Him?

In almost every home in America and other countries around the world, families have some kind of defense strategy, should they need to defend themselves. Just take a look around at what's happening in our society today. Some defense tools include guns, bats, knives, and sledge hammers, but there are many different defensive or even offensive tools. Many families take extra measures to protect themselves from others, such as using fences or bodyguards or learning tae kwon do. All these are implemented in the name of protecting self and loved ones.

If you look through history, you will notice that everyone has something, even though they are not sharing that information. Many take classes to perfect their ability to use strategies or resources to defend themselves. Guess what? As we evolve, new strategies or tools emerge, and we go after them, even though some can't afford it. Some suggest, "Why not borrow money and charge them on your credit card?" You keep getting yourself deeper in debt with an unrealistic sense that you will pay it off. Oh, how we abandon the old and chase after the new so easily.

The best weapon to safeguard us, both physically and spiritually, which has remained constant in our lives, is the Bible. We take precautions to ensure that we stay alive, but what do we do to ensure our lives are secured spiritually as well? The Bible. All these man-made weapons will protect us only by physical means. The Word of God will protect us from both physical and spiritual means. I think that more than 80 percent of families in America own a Bible, but there is a difference between owning a Bible and studying it.

No one can utilize his or her free will effectively without utilizing the Bible properly. The Bible is the best physical and spiritual weapon ever assembled, straight from God to humankind. We cannot exist or function, as God ordained us to do, without it. We have to learn how to use it on a regular basis, just as we master how to use man-made weapons for our protection.

Self-care is not just nurturing yourself with your physical needs. Your spiritual needs deserve to be nurtured as well. We cannot live by bread alone (Matthew 4:4); humans cannot live by healthy food or exercise alone. With the knowledge and implementation of what the Bible says, wishes of evil against you will not succeed.

> "No weapon forged against you will prevail, and you will refute every tongue that accuses you. This is the heritage of the servants of the Lord, and this is their vindication from me," declares the Lord. (Isaiah 54:17)

We are on a warfront, both physically and spiritually, with Satan—every single second of the day. Satan doesn't sleep and never gets tired. His one and only goal is to squash the good characteristics of our free will, ordained to us by God. Satan's desire is not to destroy or eliminate it from humankind. His intention is to fashion it for his evil crusades against us and against the will of God. How can we comprehend the severity of this matter and know how to fight back effectively?

Let's examine what the Bible says.

> Finally, be strong in the Lord and in his mighty power. Put on the full armor of God, so that you can take your stand against the devil's schemes. For our struggle is not against flesh and blood, but against the rulers, against the authorities, against the powers of this dark world and against the spiritual forces of evil in the heavenly realms. Therefore, put on the full armor of God, so that when the day of evil comes, you may be able to stand your ground, and after you have done everything, to stand. Stand firm then, with the belt of truth buckled around your waist, with the breastplate of righteousness in place, and with your feet fitted with the readiness that comes from the gospel of peace. In addition to all this, take up the shield of faith, with which you can extinguish all the flaming arrows of the evil one. Take the helmet of salvation and the sword of the Spirit, which is the word of God. And pray in the Spirit on all occasions with all kinds of prayers and requests. With this in mind, be alert and always keep on praying for all the Lord's people. (Ephesians 6:10–18)

This is what we are fighting against. It's a great idea to buckle up, spiritually. There will be a lot of spiritual "turbulence." We are not God's instruments for only what we can see, feel, hear, or touch. We are being used for what we cannot see, feel, hear, or touch.

Sometimes, you will feel physically exhausted, which could stem from a spiritual battle you may not even realize you participated in. Even though your physical body may be resting or doing something, your spirit is still active and participating in spiritual warfare. As Paul explained in 1 Corinthians 5:3, "For my part, even though I am not there physically, I am with you in the spirit."

> For though I am absent from you in body, I am present with you in the spirit and delight to see how disciplined you are and how firm your faith in Christ is. (Colossians 2:5)

You will feel worn out at times, but you'll have no idea why. If you want to find out more, read your Bible constantly, and more will be revealed to you. The only way we can replenish our energy is by praying constantly and touching base with God consistently through His Word. It goes beyond that.

> For though we live in the world, we do not wage war as the world does. The weapons we fight with are not the weapons of the world. On the contrary, they have divine power to demolish strongholds. (2 Corinthians 10:3–4)

If the Lord is a warrior, so are you (Exodus 15:3). You did not become a born-again Christian to just hang out with Christians.

Do you know how Satan wants you to find a needle in a haystack? By stepping on it. God's plan for you through His Word is to prevent you from stepping on Satan's traps or his poisonous needles. God didn't create us in His image for nothing. He also wants us to possess all His characteristics. He wants us to understand His thoughts and feelings and the reasons behind His actions, His plans, and what's to come. While we are battling the spiritual forces of evil every second of the day in the spiritual realm, some of these spiritual battles are manifesting into battles we may actually see or feel. Some may not look like battles because they are disguised by Satan. Also, some may appear as if we did something wrong, and God is punishing us. These are all Satan's doing. His crusades are to make God look like everything God is *not*, in order to elevate himself and cause both spiritual and physical havoc (John 10:10).

You will know if the challenging circumstances are coming from the evil one, caused by your actions (by deviating from God's path), or a test of your faith (obedience). Satan is a counterfeit. He tends to disguise himself to appear as if God is speaking to you, and he appears to be equal to God. Don't let Satan snatch you away. Discern! Discern! Discern! (John 10:27; 2 Corinthians 11; Ephesians 4:27). While I won't be able to touch on every factor, I will explain a few. You'll be able to connect the dots for yourself after I share my thoughts.

Satan plots and set traps, but God disarms, thereby clearing the way for us. Remember this phrase: *blessing in disguise*. God uses many approaches to intervene for us every second of the day. We may not see some of His interventions in ways we assumed we would. We might feel very frustrated, angry, disappointed, or depressed, but we need to thank God for whatever He did.

We need to trust God because he always has our best interest in mind. He always has our backs (Psalm 91). A lot of evil activities happen behind our backs or behind the scenes—even in front of us—that we can't even imagine. Much spiritual warfare is going on, but we are oblivious. That's where we fall short; we do not see the traps that Satan sets, but God sees them and blocks them.

Digest this section slowly: I have great neighbors. The two who are very close to me are Pete and Sherry. About two years ago, Sherry went for a drive to Titusville to drop off something. On her way home, her fairly new car broke down. She was stranded for about two hours or so. Pete had to leave his job to go help her. She described what happened—it was a rough day.

I asked, "What if God intervened? What if your car broke down to prevent something fatal from happening to you? What if it wasn't about you but about Pete, who left his job the moment he heard that your car broke down? What if God prevented something from happening to him by pulling him out of whatever he was doing at that same moment? You just never know." I know, however, that God is always ahead of Satan.

I have another story to share. A couple with whom I am very close, Josh and Kara Van Zandt, informed me about three encounters they had relating to accidents. In three consecutive months (one accident per month), someone backed into their cars and damaged them. Of the three incidents, two were Josh's car and the last incident was Kara's. Kara said that she was at peace during these incidents, and they took their cars to be fixed after the third accident. I knew for sure that God was up to something and that God's hands were behind these incidents.

I thought, *What if God was disrupting Satan's plans to cripple this family?* Each time Satan shifts his goalposts or traps, God throws in a hindrance or intervenes.

Sherry told me a story of an incident after Hurricane Ian struck Florida. A family's house was flooded due to the hurricane. Servpro came to do a repair estimate, after which the family left the house, but the wife decided to go back to the house to get something. When she got there and opened the door, there was smoke in the home. Imagine if they had left loved ones at home? We have to understand that Satan's scheduled plans or traps against the children of God are very messy and chaotic. This is because he wants those traps to be difficult to track—but it's impossible to deceive his Creator.

Have you ever wondered why it took so long to check out of a grocery store, been stopped by a police officer on your way to work, taken a wrong exit, or gotten sick all of a sudden so you couldn't attend an event? What if God was preventing something you could not visibly see, feel, or notice? Think back about certain things that happened in your life that God could have been behind. Take a deep breath and think about this. God is at work all the time. Are those hindrances directly from God? They could be. If Satan can't win you over, he wants to destroy you or send a wave of chaos as much as possible in your life.

Remember everything that Joseph's brothers did to him and how he finally told them who he was and that it was God's plan all along?

> Then Joseph said to his brothers, "Come close to me." When they had done so, he said, "I am your brother Joseph, the one you sold into Egypt! And now, do not be distressed and do not be angry with yourselves for selling me here, because it was to save lives that God sent me ahead of you. For two years now there has been famine in the land, and for the next five years there will be no plowing and reaping. But God sent me ahead of you to preserve for you a remnant on earth and to save your lives by a great deliverance. (Genesis 45:4–7)

> "You intended to harm me, but God intended it for good to accomplish what is now being done." (Genesis 50:20)

How could his brothers do such things to him? Could we look at a situation and say, "It's the will of God that such things are happening"? It's hard to swallow, right? There's another thing God does that doesn't appear to make sense, but it makes sense after all. God protects and saves! Then again, many families have loved ones who didn't make it back home for one reason or the other. My condolences. May God continue to be your comfort and refuge. Never lose hope.

Another way that Satan attacks children of God is through their families. God ordained three institutions—the government, the church, and the home. Of these, the home is the most powerful. The home is where everything originates. The church is the bride of Christ, and each family makes up the church. In fact, the home makes up the government as well. Therefore, the home is the biggest threat to Satan. God wants each family to be fruitful, multiply, and fill the earth and subdue it, as referenced in Genesis 1:28. Satan, however, plans to work against every one of God's intentions. Due to this fact, Satan constantly pretends that he wants us to be fruitful, multiply, and fill the earth, but he wants each home to subdue the other in evil ways, such as lies, violence, deception, and mistrust. Satan is severely troubled—I say he's lost his mind—because the Bible is safeguarded, taught, understood, mastered, and applied in each person's life in each Christian home. Satan fully understands that doing so will result in each family's morals and values being aligned with the scripture. This powerful institution, home, is a priority to God, as He wants to continue to breathe His Word on families so they may keep growing and get stronger.

Home is also Satan's priority—but for destruction. Christian families are on Satan's destruction shortlist. Satan's plan is to sow as much dissension, mistrust, violence, addiction, control, and dark secrets as possible in order to uproot and deter each family from aligning their lifestyles with the scripture. Satan tirelessly continues to introduce fatal options to families that contradict the scripture and remove God's name from their sight and minds. Satan's desire is to incapacitate each family's ability to recognize God as their Savior and refuge. Remember the verse from Mark 10:9—"Therefore what God has joined together, let no one separate." Satan despises that verse more than you could ever imagine. The words *joined* and *together* are words Satan works tirelessly to destroy to result in the opposite effect. Satan's strategy? Go after the minds of individual family members in order to poison them, which would result in chaos.

Why would Satan want to attack your mind? Because your mind is the part of the image of God where God communicates with you and reveals His will to you. (Wiersbe 1979, 10)

How does each family combat Satan? Pray together, pray individually, read God's Word together, read God's Word individually, keep your mind on track through His Word, and constantly examine the Bible to ensure what you are hearing, feeling, and seeing matches the scripture. There will be a lot of temptation thrown your way. Remember that all the children of God, both in the Old Testament and New Testament, were tempted. The author and finisher of our faith, Christ Himself, was also tempted in many ways. If you can control your mind through the scriptures, however, your true self and your free will be aligned with God's desires.

Human beings are filled with drama. When you purchase a product, it has a tag on it. Human beings' tags read, "Drama." Unfortunately, consciously or unconsciously, we create dramas by the decisions we make, and we expect God to fix it. If we lean on our own understanding, we will create more than we expected. It doesn't go well. We get very frustrated, to the point that some people stop engaging through His Word or praying. We have the habit of deviating from God's tracks, thereby creating firestorms in our lives. We create self-inflicted wounds. Then, we wonder why God is not doing anything.

Trust in the Lord with all your heart and lean not on your own understanding; in all your ways submit to him, and he will make your paths straight. (Proverbs 3:5–6)

Self-inflicted wounds occur when an individual refuses to trust God by engaging in acts that God did not ordain. Our understanding is very skewed, even though it may appear to be a smart or intelligent decision. There is no doubt we are going to battle ourselves, but there were times when I wondered and said, "My goodness! Why in the world did I do that?"

In his book, *Higher Is Waiting*, Tyler Perry (2017) states,

Acknowledge the pain, but then try to take a few steps away so you can get some distance. Once you have space, try to look at your situation more clearly, without your reactive mind. Try to change your perspective. See how your present circumstances can work for your own good. It will. Once you do this, see how your predicament can be used as nourishment for your growth. Ask yourself, "Why did this happen? What's my part in the chain of events? How would I do it differently next time? When you arrive at the answers to the questions, it will be easier for you to accept what happened, forgive, recover, and move on." (109)

When I was in Nigeria, one of my friends told me a story. I was not sure where the story originated, but over the years, I realized it was meant to be allegorical. Here's that story:

A man had ten rooms. He decided to give Christ five rooms. When Satan showed up and knocked, he attacked the man, and the man screamed for Christ, but Christ did not come to rescue him. The next day, the man asked Christ why didn't He come to his rescue.

Christ responded, "You only gave me five rooms to safeguard."

The man decided to give Christ two more rooms. Satan repeated the same behavior, and the man screamed Christ's name for help, but He did not answer. The next day, the man asked Christ the same question, and Christ gave him the same answer: "You gave me only seven rooms to safeguard."

The man decided to give Christ all ten rooms. When Satan showed up again, it was not the man who answered the door. It was Christ.

Immediately, Satan bowed down and said, "I've knocked at the wrong door." Then, he fled.

One simple allegory; one simple logic and truth behind the allegory. We cannot expect God to work on our defense when we withhold some areas of our lives that we do not want to give to Him. Our hearts and consciences need to be handed over to God. With God, not everything goes. There are a lot of distractions and noises in our world today. We crave things over which we have no control, or we chase after things that would draw our focus away from God. Earlier, I referenced Galatians 5:13—that "we should not use our freedom as an opportunity for the flesh." When our desires are not aligned with God's desires, we set ourselves up for failure and suffering. The best step to take and maintain is to avoid shooting ourselves in the foot.

Just because the world changes its ways by pushing Satan's desires does not mean God's Word will adjust to fit in. God will not change His patterns just because we chose a route that He does not approve, ordain, or condone. Beware of those routes that provide you with instant gratification but will result in more harm than good. So, what's the solution? Two passages came to mind:

> Search me, God, and know my heart; test me and know my anxious thoughts. See if there is any offensive way in me, and lead me in the way everlasting. (Psalm 139:23–24)

> Examine yourselves to see whether you are in the faith; test yourselves. Do you not realize that Christ Jesus is in you—unless, of course, you fail the test? (2 Corinthians 13:5)

Other passages may cross your mind that you can apply here as well. Have total surrender by letting God take the wheel over your heart and home. By doing so, when Satan knocks, he will realize that he knocked at the wrong door.

I cannot tell you of a child of God who was not trained or tested by God when reading Genesis through Revelation. While God tests or trains His children, Satan tempts God's children. God is always faithful and trains or tests us constantly. His training or tests (past, present, and future) are to ensure we are anchored down with faith and obedience to Him alone. He shapes us and strengthens us, and He makes His presence known through those training. Satan, on the other hand, tirelessly tempts or challenges us every minute in order to see us fail and disobey God's guidelines.

When God is training you, you will know. When Satan is tempting you, you will also know. Why? Because you have a discernment spirit (Romans 12:2; Philippians 1:9–10; 1 John 4:1). In fact, some people possess discernment of the Spirit (1 Corinthians 12:10). There is training for every job under the sun. Training is meant to be used to sharpen your knowledge about that particular job you do. There may be quizzes after each training. A lot of people fail because they choose to distance themselves from participating in training. Sometimes, the end result is that they are let go. Trust me on this—you will go through a lot of spiritual training (tests and temptations) because you are a member of God's family. Acknowledge it as "Training Day." There is no exception to this matter. A few children of God were tested—Abraham (Genesis 22); Joseph (Genesis 37–50); God allowing Satan to test a child of God (Job 1–14); Shadrach, Meshach, and Abednego's challenge (Daniel 3); and Daniel's challenge (Daniel 6). Another example is that we think so much of ourselves. That is the part the Holy Spirit plays. A lot of powers and unmeasurable wisdom have been bestowed upon us. Sometimes, we get cocky and start thinking we are above reproach.

Two prime examples are King Uzziah and King Jeroboam. Satan infested their hearts and consciences, which led to skewed leaderships. Uzziah became very powerful and arrogant and walked into the temple to burn incense, which was the priests' job. His behavior resulted in his having leprosy until the day he died (2 Chronicles 26). Lesson learned? Yes! We should always stay in our lane and concentrate on the gift God gave us. You have to be called to step up to the plate for the work that God ordained you to do. Second,

King Jeroboam allowed Satan to invade his thoughts, which led him to lean on his understanding, instead of God's. He formulated a plan that seemed very wise and strategic in order to remain in power. He built idols around his territories to prevent anyone from going to Jerusalem (1 Kings 12). It backfired. The prophet Ahijah, who gave Jeroboam the good news that he would become a king, was the same prophet who gave him the bad news about the kind of death his family would face due to disobeying God (1 Kings 14). Lesson learned? Yes! If we suppress the Spirit in us and don't discern every thought that flows through our minds, we will appear to be like people who make coffee without filters. We would not like the taste, which is the result of the path or decision we chose to make. Some thoughts may appear to look great, but is the thought from God? Stay on a narrow path, not the wide path (Matthew 7:13–14).

The earth is infested with diseases. Satan can also strike us with all kinds of illnesses to disable our ability to stay focused on God. I wonder why God allows such illnesses to happen to loved ones. This is very difficult to swallow. I sympathize and pray that God watches over you and your loved ones. I pray that He may comfort you, give you strength, and give you peace as you and your family go through sufferings.

God, however, is always ahead of Satan. Jesus's gruesome death on the cross comprises more than we know. God is our healer, but he was pierced for our transgressions. He was crushed for our iniquities. The punishment that brought us peace was on him, and by his wounds we are healed (Isaiah 53:5). What about Peter and the other apostles or disciples who used every opportunity, when arrested and thrown in jail, to share their testimony? (Read the book of Acts and other books in the New Testament.)

If Christ was tempted and tested throughout His life on earth (Matthew, Mark, Luke, and John), we will be tested and tempted as well. Even the blind man whose eyesight was restored defended Christ, although he did not know exactly who opened his eyes. He stood by the fact and never wavered that Jesus put mud on his eyes, he washed, and then he started seeing (John 9:15). Fate—whether it comes from God, from Satan, or God allowing Satan to challenge you—will shake your core foundations and put everything you believe on the line. Never give up or give in. View it as a training day. Satan is the one who will give up or give in. He has nothing to do, other than roam the earth and constantly seek how to do the most damage.

> Dear friends, do not be surprised at the fiery ordeal that has come on you to test you, as though something strange were happening to you. (1 Peter 4:12)

You will hear, feel, and see a lot of distracting, contradicting ideas and noises along your walk with God that are intended by the devil to push you off God's track. Remember, you always have to watch and pray. Your free will, given to you, was meant to be utilized to honor God, who also equips you for physical and spiritual warfare (what the eyes can see and what the eyes cannot see). There are several reasons why God gave us so much power and authority through our free will. It's sad that many of us are not ready or even aware of the responsibilities God gave us. Some have acknowledged those responsibilities but have no desire to fight; they are always in flight mode. If God gave us the power and authority to be fearless, we are fearless indeed and always ready for battle. There is no room for fear in any way, shape, or form.

> People who suddenly find out that they are in the midst of a cosmic conflict often have one of two extreme reactions: fight or flight. Those who flee do so because they don't feel up to the task. Those who are ready to jump into the fight do so because they feel strong enough to handle it (...). There is power available, and it's the greatest power in the universe. The only way to win this was to be strong in the Lord—in the strength that Paul spent most of Ephesians assuring us is already ours. (Ingram 2006, 26)

In chapter 1, I said that you must walk across the barriers you despise to achieve your life-on-earth destiny. That is not the same as your spiritual fate and destiny because you possess it already and should simply claim it. Our human nature has a lot of flaws. Spiritually, we consistently apply our free-will manual (Bible) daily. We have to utilize the power and authority behind our free will to fight, fight, and fight. Satan has nothing more important to do than to drag us down. He's so confused that he cannot settle down with one identity. He despises his identity as the evil one, which is why he disguises himself in personalities he is not, such as the sheep, then shepherd, and then something else. God's identity is constant. Christ's identity is constant. The Holy Spirit's identity is constant. Do you know what else is constant? The "sheep"—and the *sheep* are us.

> Be alert and of sober mind. Your enemy the devil prowls around like a roaring lion looking for someone to devour. Resist him, standing firm in the faith, because you know that the family of believers throughout the world is undergoing the same kind of sufferings. (1 Peter 5:8–9)

God made it clear to us that when we submit to Him, we have the power and authority to resist the devil, and there is no doubt that he will flee. Remember—submit first before you resist. It is not the other way around. We are heroes so far; we utilize our free will biblically (Romans 8:37), limited to Exodus 3–4; 1 Samuel 17; Jonah 1–4; Acts 21; and Luke 14:25–34.

Song: "More Like You" by Clay Crosse

CHAPTER 6

LOVE AND RELATIONSHIPS PATHWAY

"I Still Haven't Found What I'm Looking For" (U2 cover, featuring Peter Hollens)

Pursuit of Love in Wrong Places and Approaches

What exactly does *love* mean? The *Oxford Dictionary* (2008) defines love as having a "strong affection towards another person or thing."

Relationship is the connectedness between two or more people or things. When I was growing up, the first genuine love I received originated from my parents, especially my mother. My mother taught me everything I know. She taught me everything I needed to know about love and relationships before her passing in 2005. Sadly, not everyone is as lucky or blessed as I was growing up. A lot of people have devastating upbringings from their families of origin.

Our family of origin plays a huge role in how we act or react to relationships. Everyone learns about love and relationships from somewhere, but a lot of people do not know the origin of it. Some do know and profess it, and some know but take it for granted. Countless movies, shows, and books about love and relationships have missed the mark. Human beings cannot live without love and relationships, but when they are portrayed inaccurately, it always results in heartbreak. A lot of things we watch on television make love and relationships look cheap, to the point that many people replicate the same strategies, which leads to disastrous outcomes. Some people just long to be loved.

Everyone deserves to be loved and cared for, but some continue to seek it where they cannot find it. Some have spent hundreds or thousands of dollars with an intention to find love and a relationship. On November 2, 2022, Fox News reported that a Minnesota woman, age twenty-eight, was gunned down in front of her work office for rejecting a coworker's advances (Rosenberg 2022).

I heard about a story reported by Jess Thompson through *Newsweek*'s e-newspaper that someone sent thousands of dollars to someone who claimed to be stuck at the space station and needed the money to pay his way back to the earth. I am not laughing at or judging the victim. Many us have done something extreme to earn someone's love. If this applies to you, I am sincerely sorry that it happened. This is not a laughing matter. I am just trying to illustrate how people, including me, have lost track of what really matters in pursuit of fraudulent love. Love and relationships have taken us to many parts of the world and made a lot of people do things they never thought they would do, all in the name of love.

Pursuit of love has fooled and embarrassed a lot of people. During the pursuit, we overlook the most important links. Unfortunately, and regardless of your financial standing, money cannot buy you love. Love is not fraudulent, a lie, disastrous, deceptive, or violent. Love is true, sincere, gentle, and amazing. You just need to comprehend the two links in order to feel whole and complete.

When you listen to other people's stories about their hunt for love and relationships, align what they are saying with their body language, and you will notice how lonely, hurt, and desperate they are to find love. They are willing to go above and beyond to find something so priceless and amazing as love. Many of us, however, look in the wrong places. We are missing the two crucial links. Have you ever gotten into a vicious cycle, where everyone you meet looks attractive and appears to be *the one?* You repeat the same act every single time and get disappointed every single time.

I have listened to a lot of people share their stories of how their loves started and how they ended. Many say they felt they had to have it right then and there. Some people chase love in order to feel complete. The more they chase, the more they get desperate. The more they get desperate, the more they violate their morals and values in the process. Still, those crucial links are missing. As a result, they hit a dead end again and again. The sad part is that even though some people knew they were being taken on a ride—abused or taken advantage of in many ways—they still ignored the signs before their eyes.

> The world's crisis is twofold. First, no one seems to know how to keep love alive, how to keep
> the flame lit, the fire burning. Second, everyone seems to be stepping out of his or her true love.
> (Evans 1995, 19)

Love doesn't have to be complicated, expensive, rough, wasteful, confusing, hateful, or chased. Wait for that *link* to be explained.

The way that love and relationships are portrayed on television shows and in books and movies are just acting and fantasies. In reality, love and relationships are not acting. They are real and deep. Have you noticed that love and relationships can go from one extreme to the other, such as from extreme love to extreme apathy? Many ignored the clues and hints revealed to them during the excitement phase—that it was a very bad idea or it wouldn't work. They moved forward anyway because of how they felt at that very moment. One snap of a finger, love is there; another snap, it's gone. Then the cycle repeats over again, all in the pursuit of love and relationship. Many act on impulse and can't seem to find themselves or know who they are in the process. Any love and relationship built on the sand will never withstand the wind. Once the wind blows at it, everything is destroyed.

Society has not made it easy. Many people are misguided by love and relationships, based on how society portrays these subjects. The factors presented by our society regarding love and relationships are very misleading. The sad part of the dilemma is that our society refuses to amend its belief systems or change its perceptions and tone. Why? Because people do not want to be discredited or appear to look incompetent. Well, that's the problem. There is nothing wrong with taking a U-turn when you know you are wrong. Skewed perceptions about love and relationships are dangerous and, in some cases, fatal. Love and relationships cannot be viewed only from the surface point of view. It is very deep and can only be understood from the link (which I will introduce to you soon). Without that one link, it's impossible to feel loved or give love. If you go by what society presents to us, you will fail.

Many of us have skipped one basic understanding about love and relationships—that it never lasts. It has led many to feel disappointed, discouraged, depressed, disgusted, and, in some cases, wanting their freedom back. This is triggered by skewed perception or lack of knowledge about love. There are a lot of misconceptions about the meaning and origin of love, which has caused havoc in many lives today. Many have run out of energy and have no desire to move forward. Many people are in the fast-paced lane of life, which also makes it impossible to find love or have a few seconds to learn and process what it really means. (Connect the missing link dot).

Love becomes a decision that is made from lack of impulse control. You dive headfirst and by the time you know it, everything else around you goes south or gets caught in the spider's web. I will say that many documentaries are true stories about love, shown in realistic fashion, and were inspirational to others. How can we apply love in relationships without being about to include the missing link? Not understanding the root and meaning of love and relationships is like operating a machine you have no knowledge about. You cannot understand it unless you invest your time and energy properly. Even if you spend a lot of time and energy learning about them, you will not understand them unless you're willing to learn them from the right source.

There are many people today whose hearts are broken in pieces, torn or lost emotionally, because of these two subjects, love and relationships, which we were created for. Think about the next statement for a minute. A lot of things we do require education or certification. We are willing to spend thousands of dollars to attain an education or certification in different professions in order to make it through life, but we are not willing to make any sacrifice to understand one simple link. You don't have to attain a doctoral degree to be called "Dr. Love" or to know what it really means. Even then, you may be missing that link.

We tend to spend a lot of time on many activities so we can prosper, but we fail to learn and understand the most critical subjects, ordained to humans by God. Love and relationships do not have to be difficult. They can be very simple to learn and master appropriately in order to have healthy relationships. I see love and relationships as the most misunderstood subjects in the universe. With skewed perceptions, love can become a destructive force. With the right perception in mind, however, it can be unequivocally the most powerful, supportive, priceless, precious, magnificent force in your life—when it's understood and applied properly. You just need to understand the basic steps about love in order to give and accept love. It is never one-sided, and it's never too late. If your intent to love is to get what you want and how you want it—not reciprocal, as the world loves—then love is not meant for you, and you will not find it.

The Two Missing Links

Song: "Love God Love People" by Danny Gokey

> Jesus came into this world for one purpose. He came to give us the good news that God loves us, that God is love, that He loves you, and He loves me. How did Jesus love you and me? By giving His life (…) The whole gospel is very simple. Do you love me? Obey my commandments. (Mother Teresa and Moore 2002, 21)

We are created to love and be loved (relationships). If you are willing to do whatever it takes to find love, then listen to what I have to say. It is imperative that you learn the origin and the pricelessness of love and relationships in order to love and be loved to the fullest. You can only learn and understand straight from the Bible. When you read through the scriptures, you will find that love found you already. Truly, God is love and the author and inventor of love and relationships.

> It is important to understand that God's love for us is rooted in His image. Not in ours. God's love flows out of His nature and His character. (Tozer 2020, 28)

I was destined and proud of my roots here on earth, but even before I was created and before my family loved me, God loved me first. Human love will end someday, as each person's life on earth is limited, but the love of Christ will endure forever. Therefore, take some time out of your day to examine this amazing book called the Bible; it's the right source and will help you comprehend what being in love and having long-lasting relationships are all about. There are numerous things that many people are reluctant to know, or they know but take them granted. One of those subjects is about God's amazing love for humanity. We pursue happiness and success in many ways, shapes, and forms. Many have sold their souls to find love, when the love of God found them first at the cross of Calvary. Without full acknowledgement of what God did on the cross, it's impossible to find everlasting love. We will continue to float around the earth.

> This is what the Lord says, he who made the earth, the Lord who formed it and established it—the Lord is his name: 'Call to me and I will answer you and tell you great and unsearchable things you do not know.' (Jeremiah 33:2–3)

This is the reason chapters 4 and 5 in this book are so significant. They lay out steps and responsibilities we must accept to be reconnected with our Father, who is in heaven. Doing so will enable the Spirit of God to live in us, who then will also reveal those unsearchable things that we do not know. It boils down to one word: love. There are many trusted lay ministers within your local churches who can help you understand love and relationships from God's perspective. Sadly, we have allowed society, the things we see on the screens, and the things we observed while growing up to indicate what love looks like and should feel like. Those approaches modeled out in the open for everyone to see are misleading. Why haven't they worked in our favor? The answer is simple. It is because we are seeking them where we cannot find them. We are not concentrating on what matters most—that Christ died for us because He loves us dearly.

Do you acknowledge that He lived in dissonance so we can live in harmony? More so, we are constantly applying the same skewed beliefs or practices that have not worked in our favor, which can be considered as insanity—repeating the same behavior and expecting a different outcome. You deserve to be in a sane love/relationship, not insane relationships. In order to attain a sane love in relationships, allow me to explain those missing links to you.

Many people in this world, including me, promised we would die for someone we loved. When the time comes, however, we use them as shields to preserve our own lives, metaphorically speaking. Any thoughts cross your mind about this statement? The only one being who made this promise and fulfilled it was Jesus Christ. Review chapter 4, "Spiritual Type and Pathway," of this book again. Still, death cannot hold Him down.

> For Christ's love compels us, because we are convinced that one died for all, and therefore all died. And he died for all, that those who live should no longer live for themselves but for him who died for them and was raised again. (2 Corinthians 5:14–15)

These may be difficult verses to comprehend. Let your heart not be troubled (John 14:1). Seek help in understanding these two subjects. Christ came and died for you and me because He loves us in many ways that we can never imagine.

> For God so loved the world that he gave his One and only Son, that whoever believes in him shall not perish but have eternal life. (John 3:16)

Another passage that explains it even further is John 15:13, which states, "Greater love has no one than this: to lay down one's life for one's friends." Notice that He referred to us as His "friends." What an amazing, beautiful, and glorious God! Our worldly friendships and relationships are filled with personal and selfish motives, but Christ's motive behind His love for us is pure. I do not want to rehash chapters 4 and 5, but if you study these passages presented to you thoroughly and with someone very knowledgeable with the Bible, you will notice that God jumped through many hoops to show and prove that He loves us beyond measure. Therefore, it's not like you are returning a favor to Him. No! You are doing your duty to love Him back with your whole heart, soul, and might. Therefore, to feel loved or to accept and give love, you must acknowledge that He loves you first. In addition, you must declare your love for Him in return, without any restrictions whatsoever.

Song: "Overwhelmed" by Big Daddy Weave

Now, my question is this: How can you understand the unsearchable things that you do not know unless you are guided by someone? When an angel of God advised Philip to go south, he obeyed and did exactly what he was asked to do. As he journeyed down south, he met an Ethiopian eunuch, who was sitting on his chariot, reading the book of Isaiah. As he was led by the Spirit of God, Philip asked, "Do you understand what you are reading?"

"How can I," he said, "unless someone explains it to me?" So he invited Philip to come up and sit with him (Acts 8:30–31). Reading the Bible is one thing, but understanding the unsearchable things that you do not know is another. Do not feel ashamed to ask your local ministers or lay ministers for help with these subjects. The one who is lost is the one who does not ask questions or seek help. If you have a Bible and have not read it, and you are very interested in learning, visit your local church.

> How, then, can they call on the one they have not believed in? And how can they believe in the one of whom they have not heard? And how can they hear without someone preaching to them? (Romans 10:14)

I am proud to be a member of Edgewater Alliance Church in Edgewater, Florida. Our church and fellowship with other believers (small groups) are where I get the spiritual nutrients to sustain my spiritual growth. I also attend Crossroads Free Methodist Church's small groups on Wednesday nights through Zoom. Crossroads Church in Clifton, New Jersey, is another church where the love of God is in action.

Many individuals in your church are gifted to teach you the way of God and model God's love for and to you. *Anyone* can be discipled, no matter where you are or your life's circumstances.

> When we come to Jesus, we begin to experience His love. In that very first moment, we have all of God's love, but the problem is, we can only understand so much. But as we continue to follow Him, we will begin to understand more and more of what His love is all about. (Tozer 2020, 29)

I am close to many families that I consider strong role models. Even though I admire all the members of our church, the families I have learned a lot from are the Sutliffs (Tim and Louise), the Mecks (Travis and Stacy), and the Dietrichs (Dan and Annie). There are so many great stories about these families, and I keep praying for them and other families within our church and other churches that God may continue to bless them more and more. I look up to these families and am very honored to be their friend because they not only profess Christ, but their actions also show it.

I have begun to build relationships with others whom I fully respect and feel like I could go to them anytime for prayers, questions, and fellowship. Make some time for others, and you will start growing with them. Make it about Christ, not you. You will need to plug yourself in to one of your local churches and build relationships with them. I hope that you will have only two motives in mind—to love the Lord with your whole heart, first, and then to love your neighbor.

> Hearing that Jesus had silenced the Sadducees, the Pharisees got together. One of them, an expert in the law, tested him with this question: "Teacher, which is the greatest commandment in the Law?" Jesus replied: "'Love the Lord your God with all your heart and with all your soul and with all your mind.' This is the first and greatest commandment. And the second is like it: 'Love your neighbor as yourself.' All the Law and the Prophets hang on these two commandments." (Matthew 22:34–40)

I will reiterate that one thing you should focus on is loving your Creator, the author and finisher of your faith. As you grow and learn what it means to love God and people, and as you observe others model the behavior for you, you will genuinely be capable of walking the walk, not just talking the talk.

Some children of God in other churches may introduce their church to you and want you to visit them. There is absolutely nothing wrong with visiting other churches, as we are one unit. I am not a fan, however, of some people who are too aggressive and forceful about it. I believe that what we should do is build each other up, regardless of which church you are a member. Avoid being one of the groups Paul addressed in 1 Corinthians 3. I encourage you to review that chapter again.

Remember that God gave many gifts to each of us to expand His kingdom. Some are church planters, and some were given gifts to invite others. I will never underestimate God and will never get in the way of His plan. That said, remember not to be too forceful or aggressive in the process to avoid being a stumbling block to another child of God. If God is doing wonders at your church and another is not, why don't you pray and support that other church that may be struggling to grow in His grace, instead of wanting the person to leave his or her church.

Have you really wondered if that is a good idea? Is God really behind that idea you are introducing to someone else? To me, it doesn't matter which church you attend, as long as the Word of God is preached, and we love Him and love others as He instructed us to do. Any church that preaches Jesus Christ as their personal Savior and walks that same walk as Jesus did, as a church, is a church of God. There will be times when there will be the worst-case scenario in a church, but Christ advised us to stay faithful to Him. In Matthew 23, Jesus confronted religious leaders by calling them blind guides, blind fools, blind men, hypocrites, blind Pharisees, whitewashed tombs, snakes, and broods of vipers. Still, He encouraged His children to listen to what they said but not what they did (Matthew 23:3). Any membership change is between God and that family. Avoid intruding or interjecting, and let God do what He does best. Don't take matters into your own hands. There is a way that appears to be right, but in the end, it leads to death (Proverbs 14:12).

Dear readers, always focus on what God needs you to do and be. There is a reason that you and your family are planted in one particular church by God. If your church is struggling in one way or the other, help them by making some sacrifices. Do not abandon them. Stand by them. I am speaking to you from experience. I fully understand what it meant not to stand by your church and what it means to abandon your church. I have lived it. Seek God's face, and ask Him to help you help them. You will see that God will use you to strengthen that church.

There are so many ways to support your home church—so many ways. One stands out to me, and that is your presence before God on Sundays. Some would argue that there is nothing wrong with worshipping God on Sundays at home. You can worship Him anywhere you want, but your presence before God at your church matters to God. The problem is that humans have become too comfortable where they are, just as a lot of people no longer kneel down to pray or reserve time to do so. God did not create us and Jesus didn't die on the cross for us to be too comfortable. If God is protecting and blessing you through the week, then He deserves your full attention through your local church on Sundays.

We did not join a church to worship people or just socialize. The church is the bride of Christ and must be held and respected in the highest honor. We go to church to worship and serve God in truth and in spirit. Some will share that their church members are great. That means God is at work in that church, but I also know that God is at work in your church as well. While you are listening and praising God's work through them, listen even more to what the still small voice is instructing you to do. It means the children of God at that church are forging forward with the duties God assigned them to do, and I give God the glory, alone. Again, there is no need to entice someone to join a particular church because we are one in Christ.

You are where God wants you to be, and your two duties are to love Him and to love people. Do not put your faith in people. People will always disappoint you, one way or the other. But if you keep your focus and faith in Christ, you will never be disappointed in any way, shape, or form.

> When they had finished eating, Jesus said to Simon Peter, "Simon son of John, do you love me more than these?" "Yes, Lord," he said, "you know that I love you." Jesus said, "Feed my lambs." Again Jesus said, "Simon son of John, do you love me?" He answered, "Yes, Lord, you know that I love you." Jesus said, "Take care of my sheep." The third time he said to him, "Simon son of John, do you love me?" Peter was hurt because Jesus asked him the third time, "Do you love me?" He said, "Lord, you know all things; you know that I love you." Jesus said, "Feed my sheep." (John 21:15–17)

Dear readers, this is love in action! In the end, church membership does not matter. What matters is giving God the glory wherever you are.

Everyone around you can be saved. Even the atheists and those who will persecute you, accuse you, lie about you, hurt you, and want you dead are all Christ's sheep because He died for us all. Some sheep were lost, and some were found and saved. God needs us to focus on His mission, which is to help Him save the lost. Remember, we were once lost but were found. We are to be a light to them, just as Christ is the light to us. I think we should not focus on church membership numbers. That is not what God is after. He's after saving the lost souls. Invite those lost souls to your church, and let God do the rest.

> I believe one of the bottom-line truths is simply this: If God can love anyone, and if God can accept my love for Him, then I can love anybody in the world. That is what God wants us to do. He wants to pour into my life this emotional love that has no boundaries––that flows back to Him and then flows out to people around me. (Tozer 2020, 30)

Do not forget that we are human beings, and sometimes human beings will get on your last nerve, but that doesn't mean you should leave your church. Settle whatever that was, and keep your focus on God.

God has plenty of work for you at your church where you are placed. All you need to do is ask. Help your church grow in His grace. If it's from God, then do whatever He asks you to do. In John 1, two of John the Baptist's disciples left John and followed Jesus. John was the one who told his disciple to look at the Lamb of God before they left John and followed Jesus. Sometimes, we tend to go by our own understanding, instead of the understanding of God.

A person may think their own ways are right, but the Lord weighs the heart. (Proverbs 21:2)

Keep your focus steady on the cross of Calvary and be willing to learn, and God will keep revealing to you the most unsearchable things you do not know regarding love and relationships. Then, you will understand the subjects better and be more equipped to receive and offer love to all around you.

The union, fate, and destiny of Christianity today are unwaveringly clear, stable, and powerful. It will remain so until Jesus's Second Coming. We must arise and forge forward and in unity. (Song: "A New Hallelujah" by Michael W. Smith and the African Children's Choir.) There is no hidden agenda, other than to love God first and then people, just as He loves us. It is not a secret society. We are fearlessly out in plain sight. Sometimes, we claim we love God and people, but we have many selfish or self-centered intentions in mind.

When you attempt to deal with love from the surface point of view, you will miss the deep and unsearchable truths about love that God is trying to show you. You need God's and His children's guidance to explain and model them for you. This is why small groups are crucial, as I described in chapter 4. Small groups help to polish your faith and strengthen your understanding about God's love and love for people. Through fellowship with others, God teaches and counsels us, with His loving eye on us (Psalm 32:8).

The Obstacle in between Loving God and People

The obstacle in between loving God with your whole heart, soul, and might and loving others is yourself. One of the problems with us human beings is that there are ulterior motives in almost everything we do. If you have motives for joining a church other than to love God first and then people second, then your endeavors will fail because they are not aligned with God's plan. This could be the reason why you feel stuck, uncomfortable, unhappy, unsatisfied, and conflicted. Having those feelings may result in you uprooting from the church of God to another, and another, and another. You will never be satisfied unless you make God's motives number one. If not number one, you will hit many dead ends. Do not join a church with an intention to find a life partner. You will disappoint yourself. Each church has boundaries or safety measures in place to avoid any misunderstanding about love and relationships. Go to church because you want to love God first and then your neighbors—to wash their feet, feed them, and take great care of them. With prior statements, you will not go astray. Then, you will be on your way to learning and understanding how Christ sacrificed Himself to prove how much He loves you. If you love God first and learn to love people around you second, He will fulfill your needs.

> And my God will meet all your needs according to the riches of his glory in Christ Jesus. (Philippians 4:19)

I have had my own share of impatience, unbelief, or skewed beliefs. I never succeeded while indulging myself in them. I was in a vicious cycle, but things started changing when I realized that it was not about me but all about God. Forming an alliance with yourself, against yourself, is destructive.

> There is a way that appears to be right, but in the end it leads to death. (Proverbs 14:12)

Therefore, don't self-destruct. Forming an alliance with God through loving Him first and people second is one bond no human being can break, and it will lead to a fulfilled life. I am not asking that you drop your dreams or plans. Always go to God in prayers about them. I am just asking that you keep your full focus on Jesus Christ. Allow Him to take the wheel in your life, and expect Him to bless you to the fullest. If you don't mind, listen to the song "Let Go, Let God" by Jack Cassidy. As I've pointed out, there will be many noises and distractions from different corners. The still small voice speaks to you regularly, and you must listen—only if you will listen.

> Early in the morning, as Jesus was on his way back to the city, he was hungry. Seeing a fig tree by the road, he went up to it but found nothing on it except leaves. Then he said to it, "May you never bear fruit again!" Immediately the tree withered. When the disciples saw this, they were amazed. "How did the fig tree wither so quickly?" they asked. Jesus replied, "Truly I tell you, if you have faith and do not doubt, not only can you do what was done to the fig tree, but also you

can say to this mountain, 'Go, throw yourself into the sea,' and it will be done. If you believe, you will receive whatever you ask for in prayer." (Matthew 21:18–22)

My point? Don't be a member of a church that does not bear fruits of love. Have you ever wondered why things are not going your way? Instead of blaming God, why not ask God what it would take for you to fix it? Maybe it's you, not God. Could it be that your plans are not in line with God's? You cannot serve two masters. Seek His face, and ask Him to remold you. Remove all those thoughts and feelings within you that have been tying you down continuously. I know what mine are, and I believe you know what yours are as well. Clear your mind and be still.

I think the discipline of silence should be the focus of my life. If I am going to experience the silent love of God, I need to be silent myself. (Tozer 2020, 89)

Song: "Quiet" by Elevation Rhythm

Trust Him, as He knows the best for you. Jesus wants us to follow Him, and He will make us fishers of men (Matthew 4:19). He never said to be fishers for our own personal or selfish interests. Think about this!

If, in our daily lives, we feel relatively unnoticed or powerless, the feeling is bound to affect our relationships with those around us. (Livingston 2009, 152)

God created you in His image out of pure love. You are a treasure to Him, and He loves you. With this knowledge in mind, you must stop beating yourself down every chance you get. If you stay on that path, it will be more difficult for you to love God and people, if you're not willing to love yourself. Your circumstances will always get in your way of loving God and loving His people. You are more than adequate because you are a child of God.

We are the sons and daughters of the coming King. If you doubt anything in the Word of God, you never believed anything He said in the first place. Until you start believing and recognizing that He loves you so much and knows what is best for you, every second of the day, you will not be at ease. As I was writing this, the song "Fear Is a Liar" by Zach Williams crossed my mind. You need to spend some alone time with God to figure yourself out and understand how valuable you are to Him. Doing so will help you align your will with God's will. Many concentrate on their misfortunes so that doing the work God calls them to do becomes impossible. If anything is hindering or setting you back from keeping focused on your calling, seek help right away. The work of God requires 100 percent of our attention. Every minute that passes is crucial and cannot be wasted.

As long as it is day, we must do the work of the one who sent me. Night is coming, when no one can work. (John 9:4)

Look into your emotional backpack and figure out those factors that are weighing you down. Seek help, as recommended in previous chapters. Take a short trip, if you need to. Call one of the members of your church whom you trust so he or she can take the matters to God in prayer as well. In his book *No Greater Love*, A. W. Tozer (2020) said,

I must confess that many times I get so tired of the noise in the city that I do something that may seem strange in some people's eyes. I get on a train leaving Chicago and go West for three hours. Then I take a return train for three hours back to Chicago. During those six hours, I am in one of those little rooms on the train by myself, nobody bothering me and nobody talking to me. And it is in those six hours when I am alone and silent before God that I begin to experience a fresh and a new sense of the love of God. God does not have to tell me He loves me. God's presence in my life reveals to me that which is the love of God. (88)

Your goals must be in line with God's. When your intentions are not aligned with God's, as evidenced by the fact that you are pursuing your personal goals instead of God's, it would be very difficult to get anything accomplished. This does not only apply to love and relationships; it applies in all areas of your life.

I know who God is only because I have accepted His love on His conditions. I think it is very difficult to understand God does not send His love on our conditions, but rather He has set the conditions. (Tozer 2020, 31)

We love because He first loved us. (1 John 4:19)

To understand the ingredients in love, review 1 Corinthians 13 thoroughly.

Song: "Proof of Your Love" by King & Country

Understanding and practicing the two aforementioned criteria (loving God and loving people) can be very difficult for some. God, however, always makes difficult things easy to comprehend. Some may say they believe and understand that God loves them, but they fail to practice God's love to others because they claim human beings are hard to deal with. God is easier, they say. These statements could have originated from what they experienced in their upbringings, past hurts, the media, or how society acts. There are also some who never believed in God's existence. Some would rather pursue other religions instead of pursuing the Way, the truth, and the life—Jesus Christ.

Unbelief is not a weakness or failure of the mind. Rather, it is an opinion. When we do not believe in Jesus, we have an opinion of Jesus, which prevents us from believing. (Tozer 2020, 14)

Human beings can be very brutal in nature, but some believe in Christ's love and want to have a stronger relationship with Him and the people around them. Whatever the case may be, if you are serious about loving God to the fullest and modeling or practicing God's love to others, you have His attention. So, who is your neighbor? Are your neighbors only people from your church or a church member who lives next to your house? Let's see what Jesus said:

But he wanted to justify himself, so he asked Jesus, "And who is my neighbor?" In reply Jesus said: "A man was going down from Jerusalem to Jericho, when he was attacked by robbers. They stripped him of his clothes, beat him and went away, leaving him half dead. A priest happened to be going down the same road, and when he saw the man, he passed by on the other side. So too, a Levite, when he came to the place and saw him, passed by on the other side. But a Samaritan, as he traveled, came where the man was; and when he saw him, he took pity on him. He went to him and bandaged his wounds, pouring on oil and wine. Then he put the man on his own donkey, brought him to an inn and took care of him. The next day he took out two denarii and gave them to the innkeeper. 'Look after him,' he said, 'and when I return, I will reimburse you for any extra expense you may have.' "Which of these three do you think was a neighbor to the man who fell into the hands of robbers?" The expert in the law replied, "The one who had mercy on him. Jesus told him, "Go and do likewise." (Luke 10:29–37)

That's a straight and clear answer there. Your neighbor is everyone God created.

Are relationships optional for you? The arguments from the Scripture and daily life say, "Absolutely not!" If you identify as a human being tied to community, then to deny, avoid, escape, misuse, exploit, or destroy it is to deny my own humanity. (Lane and Tripp 2008, 27)

They are referring to the Trinity. At this present time, it is difficult to help people due to scams and violence. Seeing someone stranded on the road and stopping to help could be fatal. People cannot be trusted because of some horrific experiences. A few people have shared some horrible experiences regarding their efforts to help someone they thought was in need but were scammed. Some have been robbed, physically attacked, or abused, and these problems are happening as we speak. Now, they are afraid to help. Some are blessed to not have experienced any of these problems, and some have never made any effort to help and are afraid to because of what they've seen on the news or have heard someone else say. Let's see what Jesus has to say about this. As Christians, regardless of what the situation is, we are called to do it anyway.

In John 8:42–59, Jesus revealed that He was eternal, and they tried to stone Him to death. He was just doing the work He was sent to do. When you read the Gospels, you'll see there were many times they tried to arrest Jesus or plotted and attempted to kill Him, but they never succeeded until it was time to die for all. Read John 11:1–11.

> [Jesus heard that His friend, Lazarus was sick. So He told His disciples that they should go back to Judea.] "But Rabbi," they said, "a short while ago the Jews there tried to stone you, and yet you are going back?" (John 11:8)

They were perplexed. He did respond.

> Jesus answered, "Are there not twelve hours of daylight? Anyone who walks in the daytime will not stumble, for they see by this world's light. It is when a person walks at night that they stumble, for they have no light." (John 11:9)

Imagine Paul being told by the Spirit of God in Acts 21 that the Jews would bind him and hand him over to the Gentiles. But that did not change his mind or his route. His response:

> "Why are you weeping and breaking my heart? I am ready not only to be bound, but also to die in Jerusalem for the name of the Lord Jesus." When he would not be dissuaded, we gave up and said, "The Lord's will be done." (Acts 21:13–14)

There are many prophets in the Old Testament and servants of God in the New Testament who knew that serving the almighty God wouldn't be a walk in the park. They stayed faithful to their individual calls. It was like that then, and it's like that now. Don't let anything stop you from your calling because that is exactly what the devil wants you to do. Paul used every opportunity he had to share the gospel. It was fun to just read through the Book of Acts and notate how he took over and navigated their minds through the Holy Spirit to share the gospel to them.

Throughout the scripture, God instructed some children of God to pursue missions in His name, in spite of the facts and threats on the ground. And from the children of God's standpoint, that mission was not such a good idea. As a result, they cowered. God, however, needed them to proceed, and at the end of the day, even though they were right from their perception, God protected them throughout their missions. There are many such examples in the Bible, but let's examine Obadiah in 1 Kings 18 and Ananias in Acts 9.

> As Obadiah was walking along, Elijah met him. Obadiah recognized him, bowed down to the ground, and said, "Is it really you, my lord Elijah?" "Yes," he replied. "Go tell your master, 'Elijah is here.'" "What have I done wrong," asked Obadiah, "that you are handing your servant over to Ahab to be put to death? As surely as the Lord your God lives, there is not a nation or kingdom where my master has not sent someone to look for you. And whenever a nation or kingdom claimed you were not there, he made them swear they could not find you. But now you tell me to go to my master and say, 'Elijah is here.' I don't know where the Spirit of the Lord may carry you when I leave you. If I go and tell Ahab and he doesn't find you, he will kill me. Yet I your servant have worshiped the Lord since my youth. Haven't you heard, my lord, what I did while Jezebel was killing the prophets of the Lord? I hid a hundred of the Lord's prophets in two caves, fifty in each, and supplied them with food and water. And now you tell me to go to my master and say, 'Elijah is here.' He will kill me!" Elijah said, "As the Lord Almighty lives, whom I serve, I will surely present myself to Ahab today" (1 Kings 18:7–15).

> In Damascus there was a disciple named Ananias. The Lord called to him in a vision, "Ananias!" "Yes, Lord," he answered. The Lord told him, "Go to the house of Judas on Straight Street and ask for a man from Tarsus named Saul, for he is praying. In a vision he has seen a man named Ananias come and place his hands on him to restore his sight." "Lord," Ananias answered, "I have heard

many reports about this man and all the harm he has done to your holy people in Jerusalem. And he has come here with authority from the chief priests to arrest all who call on your name." But the Lord said to Ananias, "Go! This man is my chosen instrument to proclaim my name to the Gentiles and their kings and to the people of Israel. I will show him how much he must suffer for my name. Then Ananias went to the house and entered it. Placing his hands on Saul, he said, "Brother Saul, the Lord—Jesus, who appeared to you on the road as you were coming here—has sent me so that you may see again and be filled with the Holy Spirit." Immediately, something like scales fell from Saul's eyes, and he could see again. He got up and was baptized. (Acts 9:10–18)

As you can see, both made a very convincing case before Elijah and God, but the outcome they expected wasn't the outcome whatsoever. Our perceptions are not always reality. God is in charge and will always make a way.

Song: "God Will Make a Way" by Don Moen

In some cases, the children of God face danger in the line of duty. It does not matter if you are on the mission field, praying for those on mission, at work, or at your home.

Before I can proceed, I will take a moment to honor and share with you about a man from my church who had a heart for missions. What makes this brother unique is that he was not killed by aggression of any kind, but it was his time to be taken by God while in the mission field.

I had an opportunity to speak to Shawn Richardson, who also has a heart for missions and was present when that brother passed. He shared some information with me. Prior to their trip, there were a few hindrances, and that brother's health-related matters were discussed. That brother, however, did not waver about going on that mission's trip and fearlessly asked, "What's the worst thing that could happen to me? Dying doing what I love?" That was exactly what happened. He passed on in the midst of doing what he loved most—missions. It was an honor to know that man, and I shall see him again.

On the other hand, the devil still prowls around. When you read through the scriptures, you will see that many children of God fled for their lives, as their lives were in danger. In 1 Kings 18, Jezebel was killing off the prophets of God. The threat at that time was at the climax, but some survived—thank God. But the threat never stopped from generation to generation.

The devil will not stop, but we shouldn't either, no matter what. I kept referring back to the scripture because that's where you will find the truth. When you review the Old and New Testaments, you will find that many children believe God was martyred. They include Abel, by his brother (Genesis 4), Zechariah (2 Chronicles 24), John the Baptist (Mark 6), Stephen (Acts 6–7), and James (Acts 12). Many have risked their lives for Christ's sake, and it's impossible to count them.

You might be remembering the loved ones who lost their lives in the line of duty for Christ. To my knowledge, there are more than 193 countries in the world. Christians have faced extreme violence in some of them in the past and still do to this day. A few of these countries are Nigeria (my birth country), Pakistan, Egypt, Central African Republic, Burkina Faso, Colombia, Cameroon, India, Mali, and Sri Lanka. As heartbreaking as it appears, children of God continue to forge forward regardless because they know the harvest is plentiful, but laborers are few (Matthew 9:35–38). We need to continue to pray constantly for not just those specified countries but for all so that God may continue to strengthen our endeavors to love Him, love people, and win souls for His kingdom.

Once you become a child of God, you are marked by His blood, and His Spirit is in you. Nonetheless, Satan has done the same in the worst way ever—to destroy you and everything you stand for.

Songs: "I Speak Jesus" by Charity Gayle and "Break Every Chain" by Jesus Culture

The Spirit of the Sovereign Lord is on me, because the Lord has anointed me to proclaim good news to the poor. He has sent me to bind up the brokenhearted, to proclaim freedom for the captives and release from darkness for the prisoners, to proclaim the year of the Lord's favor and the day of vengeance of our God, to comfort all who mourn, and provide for those who grieve in Zion—to bestow on them a crown of beauty instead of ashes, the oil of joy instead of mourning, and a garment of praise instead of a spirit of despair. They will be called oaks of righteousness, a planting of the Lord for the display of his splendor. (Isaiah 61:1–3)

Nothing should stop you from assisting, helping, and loving others as the Holy Spirit directs you. Your intentions should be pure when doing so, but you have to be cautious.

> He replied, "I saw Satan fall like lightning from heaven. I have given you authority to trample on snakes and scorpions and to overcome all the power of the enemy; nothing will harm you. However, do not rejoice that the spirits submit to you, but rejoice that your names are written in heaven." (Luke 10:18–20)

This does not mean we should gather people around us and have them watch us pick up a water moccasin, rattlesnake, or scorpion without getting bitten—that could be the end of your story.

> I am sending you out like sheep among wolves. Therefore be as shrewd as snakes and as innocent as doves. (Matthew 10:16)

In everything you do, do so with wisdom and discernment from the Holy Spirit, and do so in ways that would be about God's grace and not for your personal ego or goals. When you love others as God loves you, do so without restrictions, but be very cautious, through prayers and reading the scripture every day.

> We need people around us to see Christ through our work for Him and His kingdom. When we talk about people seeing Christ in us, it is not that they see Christ in us, but rather they see in us something they cannot explain. And of course, we know that to be Christ. (Tozer 2020, 88)

My prayer is for the love of God to radiate through you to the point that your light will shine, even when people persecute or accuse you. Love will pray for them, forgive them, and continue to move forward in order to accomplish God's plan and wishes. God chose you to be fearless.

> Do not be afraid of those who kill the body but cannot kill the soul. Rather, be afraid of the One who can destroy both soul and body in hell. (Matthew 10:28)

Satan will weaponize people to hold you back in order to delay the process, but God will always come to your rescue. Listen to this song: "Came to My Rescue" by Hillsong.

> No, in all these things we are more than conquerors through him who loved us. For I am convinced that neither death nor life, neither angels nor demons, neither the present nor the future, nor any powers, neither height nor depth, nor anything else in all creation, will be able to separate us from the love of God that is in Christ Jesus our Lord. (Romans 8:37–39)

My point? Just keep forging forward, regardless of what is thrown in your way, to accomplish the tasks assigned to you through Jesus Christ. Remember that everything that happens on your way to loving people is meant to happen. It is not a mistake. It's your fate and destiny. All you have to do is trust God through every process.

God's Love Is Radiating and Transferable

> Then Jesus came to them and said, "All authority in heaven and on earth has been given to me. Therefore go and make disciples of all nations, baptizing them in the name of the Father and of the Son and of the Holy Spirit, and teaching them to obey everything I have commanded you. And surely I am with you always, to the very end of the age." (Matthew 28:18–20)

Now that the two links have been revealed to you, know that they are not temporary but permanent. Once you comprehend, believe, and accept God's love, you will know exactly what He needs you to do. If you need help, it can be reached because God always takes away and plants someone in your life to guide you. Loving God and loving people are like a relay race. You learned from God and other children of God, and He needs you to share that information with others who know and do not know Him. It is not for you to keep only to yourself.

I have learned one habit from my men's group, which is that they constantly share information with one another. For example, one brother finds a book that uplifts him, and he shares it with another brother, once he's finished reading it. What a great habit. Also, in relay races, the baton can only be passed within the exchange zone, which is within twenty meters, and passers must always remain in their lanes after the pass to prevent them from blocking other runners. It boils down to the fact you must play by the rules. The Word of God is our rule book and much deeper than the physical relay race. Also, relay runners run to win a title, but our relay race is to win others to Christ and also win the crown that will last forever.

> Do you not know that in a race all the runners run, but only one gets the prize? Run in such a way as to get the prize. Everyone who competes in the games goes into strict training. They do it to get a crown that will not last, but we do it to get a crown that will last forever. Therefore I do not run like someone running aimlessly; I do not fight like a boxer beating the air. No, I strike a blow to my body and make it my slave so that after I have preached to others, I myself will not be disqualified for the prize. (1 Corinthians 9:24–27)

Once you accept God and His conditions, you become the "exchange zone" between God and those who are lost and need help. Everyone is an instrument to God and fashioned to do this. Remember that all our fingers are not equal, but still, we are the best-fashioned instrument for God. Sadly, throughout the scripture, God chose certain individuals as instruments, but they followed the wrong path. One prime example is Judas Iscariot.

I have made my share of mistakes and always am under construction. The more I read and pray, the stronger I get, and I advise you to do the same. Being the exchange zone between God and humans is a very busy intersection. We cannot be slow or sleepy. We must stay on the alert at all times by reading the scripture, encouraging each other, and praying to ensure that we do not falter but continue to maintain moral excellence

> All of us need other believers to inspire us to moral excellence. This is a matter of both encouragement and accountability. We need encouragement from others to make choices and commitments that we believe will please God. We also need others to help us follow through on these decisions with actions. Otherwise, it is too easy to waffle when things get tough, too easy to lose our "ethical edge." (Sherman and Hendricks 1987, 255)

When you *first* love God with all your heart, soul, and might, you have the ability to transmit the same love to people (neighbors).

> We can't move toward community with one another until we have been drawn into community with God. (Lane and Tripp 2008, 25)

These two commandments apply to all of us, regardless who we are, what we are, or where we are. Just as all who believed and accepted Jesus possess the Holy Spirit, we possess the ability to love as well. From our healthy or unhealthy interactions with others around us, we tend to fall in love in the process and desire to form families of our own. There is absolutely nothing wrong with that.

While my focus was to rehash the two great commandments and make it make all about Christ, it is clear from the beginning of creation that God intended for His children to "Be fruitful and increase in number; fill the earth and subdue it" (Genesis 1:28). God also laid out His instructions that we should follow at all times, as evidenced in Matthew 19 by Jesus Christ and 1 Corinthians 7 by Paul. Many other passages contain these instructions throughout the scripture between the Old and New Testaments, but the two aforementioned stood out for me.

Nonetheless, human beings will be human beings, as we tend to drift to do our own thing most of the time. I am no exception. Allegorically speaking, we would rather drive off the road or on downward slope into the woods and go for a bumpy ride, just for the cheap thrills. I thank God for coming after me. The song "Reckless

Love" by Cory Asbury came to my mind while writing this section. I am in no position to judge anyone. I am not the Lord. Jesus is, and my focus is to be involved in the community of the Trinity.

> No man should judge unless he asks himself in absolute honesty whether in a similar situation, he might not have done the same. (Frankl 2006, 48)

> This is why getting rooted in God's Word is so crucial to help guide and keep us on track with prayers and supplications to God. We cannot stand on our own without possessing Christ's wisdom.

> The beginning of wisdom is this: Get wisdom. Though it costs all you have, get understanding. (Proverbs 4:7)

Remember that you have every right to pursue love, but you also need to understand that fate and destiny can step in at any time. I've known many people who stated that they met by fate and also many who said they met through their faith in Christ. At my age, I have come to understand that what's meant to be will be. If it's not the will of God, then He has something much better for you. (There are many things on my mind to share about human love and relationships, but I will discuss them in my next book, by God's grace.)

> Be on your guard; stand firm in the faith; be courageous; be strong. Do everything in love. (1 Corinthians 16:13–14)

"Nobody Loves Me Like You" by Chris Tomlin

CHAPTER 7

THE NATURE OF THE WORLD, THEN AND NOW

Even though I walk through the darkest valley, I will fear no evil, for you are with me; your rod and your staff, they comfort me. (Psalm 23:4)

"I Am Not Alone" by Kari Jobe is relevant to this section.

In the Beginning

God saw all that he had made, and it was very good. And there was evening, and there was morning—the sixth day. (Genesis 1:31)

Read it again! *He saw all that He had made, and it was very good.* A while ago, I paused for a few minutes to focus and began picturing how beautiful God's creations were before the first human death that was reported in Genesis 4, in which Cain killed his brother, Abel. The experience did not last long. Then I realized how a human being became insubordinate, selfish, self-absorbed, emotional, jealous, envious, cunning, irresponsible, homicidal, and a liar. Unfortunately for us, God sees everything, and nothing can be hidden away from Him.

Nothing in all creation is hidden from God's sight. Everything is uncovered and laid bare before the eyes of him to whom we must give account. (Hebrews 4:13)

Had Cain listened and followed God's instructions, Abel could have been alive. The characteristics of human nature always get in the way. Murdering his brother did not resolve or make up for the fact that he presented God with a mediocre sacrifice, even though he knew what God expected from him. The incidents that occurred between Cain and Abel also uncover how one misstep (sin) can lead to another misstep and another and then another in a twinkling of an eye. God, however, spared his life and kept His promises (Genesis 4:15).

Just one instruction that was violated in Genesis 3 led to a series of love/hate relationships and a fatal chain of events. Unfortunately, the first fatal relationship wasn't between someone and his neighbor or an unknown person. It was between siblings (Cain and Abel). I do not consider the incident between Cain and Abel as sibling rivalry, as there were no conflicts between them, other than that Satan, once again, invaded Cain's soul and weaponized him against his own brother. The incident between the brothers revealed God's immense love for humans and the fact He stuck to His promises, with understanding and knowledge that we are flawed.

Other violence that occurred in the same chapter was by Lamech, in apparent self-defense. Sin and violence increased, while the fear of God decreased. That said, sibling rivalry and attempts to murder family members and close associates never stopped, such as Abimelech killing his brothers (Judges 9) and David and Absalom (2 Samuel). Other types of violence exploded back then. We inherited the traits of our forefathers.

When you review Genesis 5, you will discover that God intended the earth to be a paradise and perfect, but due to self-inflicted wounds by humans on themselves, everything He created went south. Even though it seemed like sin and violence dominated the earth then, two men stood out to me—Enoch and Noah. Even though God took Enoch, He had a different plan for Noah, which was to build the ark. After Noah's construction of the ark, which was followed by 150 days of flood, God blessed Noah and his family. Then He made a covenant with them and established a rainbow as the sign of the covenant with them and the generations to come (Genesis 6–9).

Sadly, Adam's bloodline was so strong that hate and violence were impossible to eliminate. God was aware of this fact, but He forged forward to repopulate the earth.

Sometimes as I process my existence, I get very emotional and read Psalm 8:3–4:

> When I consider your heavens, the work of your fingers, the moon and the stars, which you have set in place, what is mankind that you are mindful of them, human beings that you care for them?

No one is worthy before God. I am absolutely sure I am not. Through the process of writing this book, I have asked God why He chose me to do this. I broke down many times and pointed fingers and said, "You know, God, there are many other people You could have used to do this, other than me, as I could not carry the cup that Enoch, Noah, and many others carried in Your name."

My Spirit responded and said He can use whatever or whomever He wants or needs to communicate or get His message across. He knows none of us are up to par, but He's using us anyway. He made us beautiful. He blessed us. He guides us. He protects us. He just wants or needs us to act like the beautiful and blessed that He made us. It seemed, however, that all the things He's been doing haven't been enough for us. We kept heading in opposite directions. Look around the world today.

As I was processing my thoughts with regard to this chapter, I was led to review the conversation between Abraham and God about Sodom and Gomorrah, in Abraham's attempt to save them. I recommend that you read Genesis 18–19 so you can get the whole picture.

> The Lord said, "If I find fifty righteous people in the city of Sodom, I will spare the whole place for their sake." Then Abraham spoke up again: "Now that I have been so bold as to speak to the Lord, though I am nothing but dust and ashes, what if the number of the righteous is five less than fifty? Will you destroy the whole city for lack of five people?" "If I find forty-five there," he said, "I will not destroy it." Once again, he spoke to him, "What if only forty are found there?" He said, "For the sake of forty, I will not do it." Then he said, "May the Lord not be angry, but let me speak. What if only thirty can be found there?" He answered, "I will not do it if I find thirty there." Abraham said, "Now that I have been so bold as to speak to the Lord, what if only twenty can be found there?" He said, "For the sake of twenty, I will not destroy it." Then he said, "May the Lord not be angry, but let me speak just once more. What if only ten can be found there?" He answered, "For the sake of ten, I will not destroy it." When the Lord had finished speaking with Abraham, he left, and Abraham returned home. (Genesis 18:26–33)

I realized the severity of their situation as Abraham pleaded, and God did not have to have that conversation. He did, however, and it shows how merciful He was and is to this day. Their sins were described by God as so grievous that God had gone down Himself to see it (Genesis 18:20). No wonder Christ came, died, and rose in order to heal and save us from our sins.

When you read the Bible, you will definitely understand that the outrage that was happening then is happening now. Think about this: I used to be troubled about certain things going on in the world, especially in the United States. Then my Spirit asked why I was troubled or in shock, as the things happening now happened then. Unfortunately, human beings tend to choose destructive paths. It is so easy to get distracted in our world and go off track. Some individuals have the desire to follow their own senseless and selfish paths in life. Nonetheless, it is *impossible* to find clear paths without going through the Bible. As I've said, the Bible is fate's best defense in your life.

Blessed is the one who does not walk in step with the wicked or stand in the way that sinners take or sit in the company of mockers, but whose delight is in the law of the Lord, and who meditates on his law day and night. (Psalm 1:1–2)

On November 11–12, 2022, I drove to New Jersey to visit my brother and the church I consider my family church, Crossroads Church, which took great care of me when I first came to the States. While I was between Interstate 78 and 81, I saw many beautiful mountains with fall colors. They were so beautiful that I drove slowly. While I was enjoying the mountains' beauty, all I could see was the peak and trees but not the trails. The still small voice said, "When you draw closer to them, then you can start seeing the trails." So is the Scripture. Everyone, those who believe or do not believe, see the Bible all the time, but when you actually draw closer, open it, and read it, then you will find the truth and thoughts of God. In it, God will tell you the great and unsearchable things "you do not know" (Jeremiah 33:2–3).

Song: "Touch of Heaven" by David Funk (Hillsong Worship)

Our World Today

When you look at the world we live in today, don't be alarmed. Events happened then and are still happening now. If siblings and close associates could do this to one another, imagine what outsiders or the enemies can do to you. We live in an age where the bad and ugly are viewed as good, while the good or best are viewed as bad and ugly. It's a world where negative emotions and hate are governing us. It's a world where God is put on the back burner or removed from the equation, while Satan and evil deeds run rampant. It's a world where leaders of many nations are going after the weak to overtake their lands. It's a world where common sense no longer exists, and violence and destruction are approved by leaders.

It's a world where dignity is absent, a world where people in many nations are oppressed and have become the norm. It's a world where people choose power and control over working together, with no room for negotiation or compromise whatsoever. It's a world where law enforcement has no value, and it's OK to murder those who were meant to maintain law and order. It's a world where aggression is permitted, as long as it does not happen to them. It's a world where leaders advocate for defunding law enforcement, while they hire bodyguards to protect themselves, while they watch other family members perish in violence.

It's a world, where some advocate against violence but act violently against others, and it's OK. It's a world where some people condemn certain races but build their houses within the perimeter of those races they condemn. It's a world where elected leaders know that many issues have gone south but won't speak up, but they advocate destruction in order to get votes and stay in power. It's a world where chaos dominates, and that's OK.

It's a world where no one takes responsibility for anything, and it's OK. It's a world where truth is suppressed over lies. It's a world where it is no longer OK to agree to disagree. It's a world where a lot of people have no filter and say outrageous things in public in order to be popular. It's a world where there are leaders but act as if there are none. It's a world where some leaders advocate immoral ideas in public schools, while they send their children to private schools. It's a world where many people allow politics to consume them and choose political parties over the scripture. It's a world where some people go after their opponents in order to humiliate and destroy their lives for the sake of power and control.

It's a world where some people who are very intelligent act as if they are unintelligent. It's a world where compassion and grace are lacking. It's a world where some officials who are elected to protect and serve us are the same ones leading to our demise. It's a world where some leaders expect us to do what they say but not what they do. It's a world where the media only focus on their personal vendettas and narratives against each other, instead of telling the actual truth the people need to hear.

It comes as no surprise that some children of God are advocating for the aforementioned topics. It is very sad.

Song: "Is He Worthy?" by Chris Tomlin

Christ sounded an alarm while He was on earth about persecution of His children. He stated,

Be on your guard; you will be handed over to the local councils and be flogged in the synagogues. On my account you will be brought before governors and kings as witnesses to them and to the Gentiles. But when they arrest you, do not worry about what to say or how to say it. At that time, you will be given what to say, for it will not be you speaking, but the Spirit of your Father speaking through you. Brother will betray brother to death, and a father his child; children will rebel against their parents and have them put to death. You will be hated by everyone because of me, but the one who stands firm to the end will be saved. When you are persecuted in one place, flee to another. Truly I tell you, you will not finish going through the towns of Israel before the Son of Man comes. (Matthew 10:17–23)

This is very serious, but a lot of children of God are taking this matter very lightly. We need to pray like we've never prayed before. We need to read the Word like we've never read it before. We need to fellowship with other believers like we have never done before. The more we take these steps, the more we are united and stronger than ever, not for any political parties but for God and God alone. We need to stand up for the truth, hope, compassion, and grace, just as Christ modeled for us, without fear of political repercussions or of our enemies. We will be unstoppable.

I've mentioned that the union, fate, and destiny of Christianity are stronger than ever. As I listed and identified some of the disturbing issues, other factors may have run through your mind. We, however, should not be quick to speak but quick to listen (James 1:19).

When you speak without the Holy Spirit, people around you will know, but when you speak with the power of the Holy Spirit, people around you will know, listen, and take notice. Sadly, some people blurt things out that degrade God and the persons we claim to be. God is aware of everything happening now. None of what is currently happening is a mistake. He has a plan, and soon the plan will be revealed to us. He is totally in control.

Song: "In Control" by Hillsong

Jesus, the Tie That Binds Us, Is Greater than Our Differences

You are the salt of the earth, but if salt has lost its taste, how shall its saltiness be restored? It is no longer good for anything except to be thrown out and trampled under people's feet. You are the light of the world. A city set on a hill cannot be hidden. Nor do people light a lamp and put it under a basket, but on a stand, and it gives light to all in the house. In the same way, let your light shine before others, so that they may see your good works and give glory to your Father who is in heaven. (Matthew 5:13–16)

The battle on this earth will always rage on between good and evil. In chapter 5, I touched on the three institutions God ordained—home/family, the government, and the church. I also mentioned that the home/family made up the bride of Christ, the church, and also the government.

Throughout history, family has been the most powerful institution; it's the institution that Satan and his demons put most of their energies and focus on. Why? That has been God's plan, focus, and source of the expanding of His kingdom from day one. Families are ordained by God with reproductive ability. He blessed families and required all family members to establish His morals and values, which Christ modeled for us while on earth.

A review of the history of the human race shows that families are the most attacked institution in the world by Satan and his demons. It is Satan's focus of attention, and his one and only goal is to destroy this institution. It happened in the Old Testament and New Testament, and it's happening now. What should we do? We need to start praying for each family, not only in the United States but around the world, in order to dismantle spiritual weapons that the devil has fashioned against them. If the family institution is at the top of God's list, then we should make it one of our top priorities.

The following passages in the Bible encourage me:

"No weapon forged against you will prevail, and you will refute every tongue that accuses you. This is the heritage of the servants of the Lord, and this is their vindication from me," declares the Lord. (Isaiah 54:17)

What, then, shall we say in response to these things? If God is for us, who can be against us? (Romans 8:31)

These two passages don't mean we are immune from being attacked. Those weapons will continue to come our way, but our defense shield, Christ, will divert those weapons back at Satan and his demons. Satan will never stop attacking us, and we should never stop worshipping and serving God. Other promises presented to us in the scripture stand out, and those promises should be claimed. When David faced Goliath, he presented himself as confident, knowing that God was right behind him. Here is how David responded to Goliath:

David said to the Philistine, "You come against me with sword and spear and javelin, but I come against you in the name of the Lord Almighty, the God of the armies of Israel, whom you have defied. This day the Lord will deliver you into my hands, and I'll strike you down and cut off your head. This very day I will give the carcasses of the Philistine army to the birds and the wild animals, and the whole world will know that there is a God in Israel. All those gathered here will know that it is not by sword or spear that the Lord saves; for the battle is the Lord's, and he will give all of you into our hands." (1 Samuel 17:45–47)

Imagine that! A giant, a huge sword, the scary voice of Goliath, and the strength of Goliath's army did not prevent David from forging forward. He knew the promises God made to the people of Israel, and he applied those promises in his defense.

In 2 Kings 19, Sennacherib was very conceited and said this to Hezekiah:

"Say to Hezekiah king of Judah: Do not let the god you depend on deceive you when he says, 'Jerusalem will not be given into the hands of the king of Assyria.' Surely you have heard what the kings of Assyria have done to all the countries, destroying them completely. And will you be delivered? Did the gods of the nations that were destroyed by my predecessors deliver them— the gods of Gozan, Harran, Rezeph and the people of Eden who were in Tel Assar? Where is the king of Hamath or the king of Arpad? Where are the kings of Lair, Sepharvaim, Hena and Ivvah?" (2 Kings 19:10–13)

Hezekiah did not respond to him but took it to God in prayer.

And Hezekiah prayed to the Lord: "Lord, the God of Israel, enthroned between the cherubim, you alone are God over all the kingdoms of the earth. You have made heaven and earth. Give ear, Lord, and hear; open your eyes, Lord, and see; listen to the words Sennacherib has sent to ridicule the living God. "It is true, Lord, that the Assyrian kings have laid waste to these nations and their lands. They have thrown their gods into the fire and destroyed them, for they were not gods but only wood and stone, fashioned by human hands. Now, Lord our God, deliver us from his hand, so that all the kingdoms of the earth may know that you alone, Lord, are God." (2 Kings 19:15–19)

That very night, the angel of God killed 185,000 in the Assyrian camp. Prayer works. The more we pray, the more we conquer and the more we topple Satan's plans. The less we pray, however, the more Satan regains power. We just have to believe the promises God made to us. Did passages run through your mind as you read this? He never fails us.

Another defense we have is unity.

Therefore, my beloved, flee from idolatry. I speak to sensible people; judge for yourselves what I say. The cup of blessing that we bless, is it not a participation in the blood of Christ? The bread that we break, is it not a participation in the body of Christ? Because there is one bread, we who are many are one body, for we all partake of the one bread. (1 Corinthians 10:14–17)

There are so many distractions and noises in our world today. Satan uses them to get us off track. We have to amend our lifestyles with regard to all that is happening in the world. It is very easy to get distracted. Satan has been sowing seeds of discord in the church through politics, and it seems that Satan is gaining traction through discord. Think about this for a minute: If Satan can sow seeds of discord in the church's institution, imagine what he does outside the church institution. The political atmosphere in this country and many other countries around the world has been fashioned by the devil as means of dividing us, both consciously and unconsciously. We have the absolute right to defend God's morals and values, but we must communicate in love and grace.

Some families no longer communicate with the other families with whom they once were close. They end up forming alliances against each other. I wonder if that is how God wants us to act. Many people, including me, have made a few points or thrown in their two cents about their stance. It is fair to ask if the paths we have taken since the eruption of political chaos is what God wants or needs us to do. I do not think so. I am not a judge and have no desire to be, but Jesus said,

You are the salt of the earth. But if the salt loses its saltiness, how can it be made salty again? It is no longer good for anything, except to be thrown out and trampled underfoot. You are the light of the world. A town built on a hill cannot be hidden. Neither do people light a lamp and put it under a bowl. Instead they put it on its stand, and it gives light to everyone in the house. In the same way, let your light shine before others, that they may see your good deeds and glorify your Father in heaven. (Matthew 5:13–16)

We are the light and salt of the earth. Let's ask ourselves this: Based on the approaches or strategies we use, are we doing so in love, compassion, grace, and kindness? Are we implementing the same steps Christ encouraged us to follow while He was here on earth? Have you ever wondered if it's worth it to abandon, disconnect from, or block someone or a group of people because of one or two political disagreements? Wouldn't it be better to feel at ease, instead of feeling awkward? Wouldn't it be amazing to contact someone you disconnected from many months or years ago? Is it possible that those individuals have crossed your mind, and you felt that you didn't want to throw in the towel? I will just say this to you: Christ threw in the towel by sacrificing Himself on the cross of Calvary. Don't we need to do the same for His name's sake? We cannot let the devil manipulate us into becoming what Paul spoke about in 1 Corinthians 3.

This is why we should reconsider and tread carefully with political subjects. In certain scary situations when there is a group of individuals—in the dark, on the sea, on the ground—individuals tend to hold each other's hands. Why? So that they can stay together, survive together, and not lose anyone. Those situations are now. We have to hold each other's hands in unity, despite the severity of the raging sea or the chaotic nature of the world, so none of us perishes.

The Gospels demonstrate how Christ handled lawyers, church leaders, and so on. He confronted them, but at the same time, He never closed the door behind them. He kept communication open, regardless of where they stood, for He came for the lost. Unfortunately, not all of them were saved. In the same manner, we need to rise above this by staying united no matter what. Many of the people who challenged Christ appeared to be arrogant or conceited, but He maintained His stance and reiterated many things He'd said before to them as a reminder.

Therefore let anyone who thinks that he stands take heed lest he fall. (1 Corinthians 10:12)

We cannot condone sin, but our job is to love, love, and love. If someone has crossed your mind that you miss speaking to, contact the individual by text or a call. There are many different ways for us to reach someone. We don't have any excuse not to do so. If God ordained us to be the salt and the light of the earth, then we surely need to make some changes. Do not let politics divide us, but let the love of Christ unite us.

You have heard that it was said, 'Love your neighbor and hate your enemy.' But I tell you, love your enemies and pray for those who persecute you, that you may be children of your Father in heaven. He causes his sun to rise on the evil and the good, and sends rain on the righteous and the unrighteous. If you love those who love you, what reward will you get? Aren't even the tax collectors doing that? And if you greet only your own people, what are you doing more than others? Do not even pagans do that? Be perfect, therefore, as your heavenly Father is perfect. (Matthew 5:43–48)

Remember that you will need to go through the most uncomfortable routes or paths to become who you were destined to be. Do not let pride get in the way. Christ stated,

Enter through the narrow gate. For wide is the gate and broad is the road that leads to destruction, and many enter through it. (Matthew 7:13)

We cannot fit the world's garbage or luggage through the narrow gate.

We all have had a share in making someone stumble because of our actions or the things that came out of our mouths. No one is exempt from this, including me. In some cases, apologies may be necessary. I do not like hate, discord, or watching people suffer (whether it's their fault or not)—these factors irritate me. It is depressing and heartbreaking to watch. I would prefer to see people happy, content, joyful, getting along, and living peacefully. We can make this happen.

Unfortunately, we cannot save everyone, but God still wants us to do more than just our best. Think about what I said. Pray about it. Start reaching out to people from whom you've disconnected. A lot of energy and time are wasted by harboring negative feelings. If someone in your family or an individual encourages division, be the one to stand up and say it's not right to do so. God wants us to have unity. It is very important to Him. It is our job to ensure God gets His way. This is part of the reason He created us.

I will share some passages with you. While you are reading the following passages, get on your knees and pray that God will remove the spirit of discord from your heart and replace it with the spirit of unity. If someone has wronged you, go to that person. He or she is your sister or brother. Spend more time with them, and just listen, as God wants us to listen more than we talk (James 1:19).

These are the passages for your review:

Whatever happens, conduct yourselves in a manner worthy of the gospel of Christ. Then, whether I come and see you or only hear about you in my absence, I will know that you stand firm in the one Spirit, striving together as one for the faith of the gospel. (Philippians 1:27)

As a prisoner for the Lord, then, I urge you to live a life worthy of the calling you have received. Be completely humble and gentle; be patient, bearing with one another in love. Make every effort to keep the unity of the Spirit through the bond of peace. There is one body and one Spirit, just as you were called to one hope when you were called; one Lord, one faith, one baptism; one God and Father of all, who is over all and through all and in all. (Ephesians 4:1–6)

Let us therefore make every effort to do what leads to peace and to mutual edification. (Romans 14:19)

There is neither Jew nor Gentile, neither slave nor free, nor is there male and female, for you are all one in Christ Jesus. (Galatians 3:28)

How good and pleasant it is when God's people live together in unity! It is like precious oil poured on the head, running down on the beard, running down on Aaron's beard, down on the collar of his robe. It is as if the dew of Hermon were falling on Mount Zion. For there the Lord bestows his blessing, even life forevermore. (Psalm 133:1–3)

Have you ever wondered if one of the people who crossed your path was an angel? Is it possible you have crossed paths with more angels than people in a day? When you get home one day, very exhausted, and your

Holy Spirit asks you how your day was, what would you say? You likely would have a lot to say, but it wouldn't be about politics—or would it be about politics? How we treat others matters to God.

As I've said, I am an immigrant. I am so fortunate to be in a position to create jobs for citizens of the United States of America. I am one of those immigrants who made it. Hear their cry and do something!

Song: "Make Room" by Meredith Andrews (feat. Sarah Reeves and Chris McClarney)

Key to Resolving Border Crisis

Unity is the key to resolving the border crisis. In chapter 8 of my first book, *Embracing Life: Surviving the Struggle by Learning to Embrace the Experience*, I wrote about the "Unembraceables." I described how I was treated when I got here by the citizens of this great nation. To be more specific, I referred to Crossroads Free Methodist Church in Clifton, New Jersey. I recommend that you purchase that book to help you understand my journey and how I got here, not to make money from you but for you to understand where I am coming from in this section. American values and disunity are among many other topics discussed in that chapter.

Here, I will concentrate on immigration and will continue to advocate for unity in this country. I was an immigrant, and I am who I am today because of how a small church and the citizens of this great country took care of me. The political cruelty and the way things have turned out between the Reds and the Blues are hurting the integrity of this country. We are all aware of this divide among us. Things can go the right direction, however, if the leaders of this country work together to resolve one of the major crises facing the United States.

I am very sure that both political spectrums know that the tactics used with regard to the border are not working, but neither side is willing to work together. Am I surprised? No, because nothing will ever get done with disunity. One of Satan's fruits is disunity, and it seems like he continues to gain strength, minute by minute and day by day.

This country must take care of its own citizens and their interests before caring for others from other countries. The law of the land must be upheld, which each leader has sworn an oath to protect. I will share what Christ said while He was with us. When Christ was addressing the issues related to the law of the prophets, He stated,

> Do not think that I have come to abolish the Law or the Prophets; I have not come to abolish them but to fulfill them. For truly I tell you, until heaven and earth disappear, not the smallest letter, not the least stroke of a pen, will by any means disappear from the Law until everything is accomplished. Therefore anyone who sets aside one of the least of these commands and teaches others accordingly will be called least in the kingdom of heaven, but whoever practices and teaches these commands will be called great in the kingdom of heaven. For I tell you that unless your righteousness surpasses that of the Pharisees and the teachers of the law, you will certainly not enter the kingdom of heaven.
> (Matthew 5:17–20)

I am not saying that the law should be disregarded, but I am asking for compassion, grace, hope, kindness, love, negotiation, and compromise. I am praying for our leaders not to spend a lot of energy and time crafting what to say against each other but to spend more time crafting options and discussing them with each other. The finger-pointing, discord, animosity, and hate have grown to become ivy plants that poison the heart and soul of America. The immigrants coming here are extremely desperate and need to escape from the smell of death that hunt them.

The United States is the most powerful country in the world, and it has what it takes to work together. Look at how the USA operates around the world. We are always encouraging countries in conflict to come to the table. Evidently, we still have it in us if we are advocating for other nations to do so. If that is the case, why can't we do the same at home with regard to our borders? I support the laws we have, but a lot of things have gone wrong.

It breaks my heart to see people hiding in car trunks and trailers, piling up on top of each other, barely able to breathe, and often dying in the process. I am not encouraging such behavior, but it tells me how desperate they were. Wouldn't it be great if our leaders showed the same leadership they show around the world? There is a middle ground. It will always exist. Once again, I am not encouraging immigrants to break the law; I am pointing out the significance of each side coming to the table to work on this project. I can't say what should be done, but I am absolutely sure that ignoring, finger-pointing, causing discord, and everything that goes with it will not resolve this issue. Also, we will continue to see a flock of people desperately walking, swimming, and hiding in vehicles to come into this country.

By not doing something significant, drug dealers, criminals, and terrorists will continue to take advantage of the fact that we are not on the same page. Border states are crying for help, and the current administration should listen and acknowledge the cry. We don't know what is going on behind closed doors, but we do know what's going on in front of the screens, and it is not attractive.

I will share a few of my thoughts about foreigners:

Do not mistreat or oppress a foreigner, for you were foreigners in Egypt. (Exodus 22:21)

When a foreigner resides among you in your land, do not mistreat them. The foreigner residing among you must be treated as your native-born. Love them as yourself, for you were foreigners in Egypt. I am the Lord your God. (Leviticus 19: 33–34)

The land must not be sold permanently, because the land is mine and you reside in my land as foreigners and strangers. (Leviticus 25:23)

The community is to have the same rules for you and for the foreigner residing among you; this is a lasting ordinance for the generations to come. You and the foreigner shall be the same before the Lord. (Numbers 15:15)

And you are to love those who are foreigners, for you yourselves were foreigners in Egypt. (Deuteronomy 10:19)

Do not take advantage of a hired worker who is poor and needy, whether that worker is a fellow Israelite or a foreigner residing in one of your towns. (Deuteronomy 24:14)

I encourage children of God to pray hard about this. Pray about unity. Pray about compassion, grace, love, and kindness. Pray that the leaders put their differences aside and work together to identify resources that will better assist these immigrants. If they were doing well, they probably would have no desire to show up at our borders. This is the United States of America and is not owned by the Blues or the Reds. Olive branches need to be extended. People may think I am out of my mind, but I will stick to one thing I know, and that is with God, all things are possible (Matthew 19:26).

Song: "Immigrant's Song" by Keith and Kristyn Getty, featuring Jordyn Shellhart

The Imminence of Christ's Return Is Still Intact

Remember that this was like this in the past and is still the same now. Nothing has really changed, but Christ informed us that things will get worse before His coming. The things happening now happened thousands of years ago, but we should not be afraid. Also, the fact that then and now are the same does not diminish, depreciate, or change the imminence of Christ's returning. I respect many Christian leaders who have written books about what we are facing now and how that is related to Jesus's Second Coming. In fact, I agree with them, but I will add this: *it will get worse*, dear readers. I have chosen four passages for this section:

Therefore keep watch, because you do not know on what day your Lord will come. But understand this: If the owner of the house had known at what time of night the thief was coming, he would have kept watch and would not have let his house be broken into. So you also must be ready, because the Son of Man will come at an hour when you do not expect him. (Matthew 24:42–44)

But about that day or hour no one knows, not even the angels in heaven, nor the Son, but only the Father. (Matthew 24:36)

For you yourselves are fully aware that the day of the Lord will come like a thief in the night. (1 Thessalonians 5:2)

Look, I come like a thief! Blessed is the one who stays awake and remains clothed, so as not to go naked and be shamefully exposed. (Revelation 16:15)

The word *thief* was used several times. First of all, Christ was not referring to Himself as a "thief." It was an analogy. In the context, He meant that a thief would not tell you his plan to rob anyone. The *Oxford Dictionary* (2008) defines *thief* as "a person who steals," and most prefer to do it in the dark. Some family members keep watch at night—with one eye open while they are sleeping. Christ wants us to be as alert and ready as possible, not only in the daytime but at night too and on a consistent basis.

Not every robbery succeeds. Sometimes, something goes wrong. Several factors can contribute to a failed robbery, such as being apprehended, someone sabotaging the plans, human error, or death. Nevertheless, I tell you today that Christ's return is spotless and has no error whatsoever. There are no informants or tipsters to alert you of the day or the hour of His return. Christ said that even the angels do not know, nor does He, but only the Father does. He doesn't want us to live in fear or walk on eggshells. He wants us to walk in confidence and be alert.

We should not get too comfy. We cannot stay alert on a consistent basis without Christ's help. I pray and ask God to continue giving me and you the strength to abide in Him and keep watch. We need Him to keep us on track.

Song: "Jesus I Need You" by Hillsong Worship

CHAPTER 8

ENCOURAGEMENT AND FORGIVENESS PATHWAY

Be kind and compassionate to one another, forgiving each other, just as in Christ God forgave you. (Ephesians 4:32)

Song: "Forgiven" by David Crowder

The Heart of Forgiveness

When you review the Bible, you will find multiple passages in which God or Christ made statements relating to forgiveness of the Israelites or other individuals. Christ is the author of and model of forgiveness. When Christ was in human form on earth, *all* His interactions—every one, every time—targeted rescuing their souls first. This reveals to us how highly God rated the importance of healing and forgiving our spiritual natures. He maintained His spiritual standards while in human form, and He showed what forgiveness and healing means. While in human form, He proclaimed that He was the Christ, even though many did not believe Him—they didn't believe He could do what He said, and they viewed those statements as impossible to attain. Why? It was because they were looking at Christ through their human lenses instead of through the spiritual lenses. Does this mean that humans, right from the start, understood their human limitations? Was it evident in the Gospels that some did not see Christ beyond the human mind's level.

Pause for a minute and think about this. If someone showed up out of nowhere with a huge hammer and cape and claimed to be Thor, and then he asked you to grab his hand, would you? We realize how easy it is to doubt or reject what someone claims to be. Sadly, human nature prevented them from understanding and recognizing that they were speaking to Christ, their Savior.

I thought of the hard conversation between Christ and the Samaritan woman at the well (John 4). It was that woman's fate to be at the well at that time for a heart-to-heart conversation with Jesus. He laid everything out to her. She became one of the people who saw Him beyond human comprehension. At that very moment, she saw the Messiah face-to-face and shared the great news. Prior to this interaction between Christ and the Samaritan woman, Nicodemus also had a heart-to-heart conversation about being born again (John 3–4). They seemed to make their very best efforts to understand that Jesus was the Messiah.

Jesus's conversations with both individuals showed how patient He was from start to finish. Many of us have had a conversation with someone who didn't understand the concept we were explaining. When you read those two chapters (John 3–4), you will recognize that they displayed "contrite hearts" in order to connect with Christ at His spiritual level. You might have heard the song "Humble Thyself in the Sight of the Lord." All it takes is to be humble, and He will lift you up to His level.

To understand Jesus, you must connect with Him through a sincere, contrite heart. The key to understanding Jesus is in having a contrite heart. Without possessing it, you cannot understand Him. And if you do not understand Jesus, you cannot understand forgiveness.

What is forgiveness all about? By definition, forgiveness is a person's ability to exonerate someone who has offended or sinned against that person. Christ described forgiveness as containing no condition whatsoever. In Matthew 18, Christ demonstrated to His disciples who was the greatest in the kingdom of heaven. He cautioned against actions that would lead another believer to sin. He stated the importance of going after the lost sheep and taught them the process of dealing with a believer who sinned. Right after those discussions, Peter, with a contrite heart, explored Christ's thoughts with regard to forgiving others. He asked how many times he should forgive someone who sinned against him. "Seven times?" Peter asked.

Here is how Christ responded:

Jesus answered, "I tell you, not seven times, but seventy-seven times." (Matthew 18:22)

Christ demonstrated about an unforgiving debtor. Christ presented examples to which they could relate and left no stone unturned in addressing these matters.

At one point in my life, I processed the conversations Christ had with different people about forgiveness. The way He taught and modeled it to them amazed me, and I asked myself, "Who can do this? Our human nature has a limit to how much we can tolerate certain behaviors." I doubted and said it was impossible. When I first became a Christian and was reading the Gospels, I wondered if Christ could deliver on some of the promises He made, especially regarding forgiveness, considering how brutal human nature could be. Then I remembered that it's impossible to understand spiritual matters without a contrite heart or from a human level of understanding. I read on—He was arrested, judged in bizarre ways, tortured, crucified, died, and rose again. They attacked everything He stood for, not only His human nature but His spiritual nature as well. He was in anguish from the time He was in the garden of Gethsemane to the time He was crucified. In His agony while on the cross, Jesus made these statements:

"Father, forgive them, for they do not know what they are doing." (Luke 23:34)

"Truly I tell you, today you will be with me in paradise." (Luke 23:43)

"Woman, here is your son," and to the disciple, "Here is your mother." (John 19:26–27)

"Eli, Eli, lema sabachthani?" (which means "My God, my God, why have you forsaken me?") (Matthew 27:46)

"I am thirsty." (John 19:28)

"It is finished." (John 19:30)

Even though He was in agony, Jesus did not care as much about His physical nature as He cared about His spiritual nature. Also, His human nature and human limitations did not prevent Him from being the Lamb that was slain. Why? Because the spiritual nature is eternal, while the physical nature is temporary. He experienced trauma, just like us. (Traumatic experiences include sexual, physical, psychological, and so forth.) After all He had said and done, Jesus delivered. Throughout the Gospels, He did not just *talk* of forgiveness, but He walked the walk of forgiveness.

Christ Understands Our Individual Traumas

Song: "He Understands" by Chandler Moore

As I was processing my thoughts about the extent to which Christ showed how much He loves and forgives us, I realized why it is so difficult for many people to forgive, myself included. Now I understand that some people have gone through massive, horrific, extreme, or brutal abuse from their upbringings. I cannot imagine what they went through. Over the years, I have heard the most horrible, horrific, and traumatic stories of the experiences people from different regions went through. In fact, they are still going through them to this day. This could stem from their families of origin or from current relationships. Because they never healed from their traumatic experiences, they continued to engage (consciously or unconsciously) in relationships that maintained the status quo. Sometimes, it is difficult for some people to break the cycle. They feel stuck, speechless, and desensitized. Although our human abilities are limited as to how to cope and heal from these horrifying events, our spiritual natures are present and ready to rescue us from bondage, if we let them. In our own anguish, it is hard to let go and let God.

No one should minimize what you went through. No one has lived the life you lived or suffered the traumas you experienced. Even though your emotions and physical body were battered by the abuse you experienced, and you have no desire or energy to move on, always remember that Christ understands what you are going through and will give you the desire and energy to forgive.

Many will say they are not Jesus, which is fair to say. You are not Jesus, but He wants you to take one step at a time toward forgiveness so you can be healed. He's holding your hand. He is in front of you, by your side, and behind you. He cares, and there is hope!

Throughout my career in mental health counseling, I provided counseling to families but also learned from the many things they presented to me. At times, it was difficult to listen to some stories because they had a very raw perspective. Sometimes, all they needed was for someone to listen to them without judgment. In certain situations, I could not do more to empower them. Then, I would take their stories to God through prayers.

Three stories stood out to me. In the first two stories, individuals had experienced so much trauma from their upbringing that they were not able to love themselves or escape from their vicious cycles. They struggled to settle their minds; they felt lost, did not want to live anymore, and had difficulty forgiving those who had severely hurt them. Their lives and interactions with others continued to be painful, with never-healing wounds.

Another was a woman who got into a severe car accident with her two children in the car. She was in a coma for a couple of days, and one of the children was hurt. Her mother, brother, and significant other passed away within six weeks of each other. She never stopped loving and caring for her children and stayed strong through the process. I have so much respect for her.

I listen to people share their stories with broken hearts, and they appear to not know what to do or to whom they can turn. I always know that God is not staying silent in their lives. I cannot bear all the traumatic experiences they went through, but I know who could. His name is Jesus. If this is difficult for you to bear, I will present two important verses from the scripture for you to study and to hold on tightly.

Surely he took up our pain and bore our suffering, yet we considered him punished by God, stricken by him, and afflicted. But he was pierced for our transgressions, he was crushed for our iniquities; the punishment that brought us peace was on him, and by his wounds we are healed. (Isaiah 53:4–5)

Take my yoke upon you and learn from me, for I am gentle and humble in heart, and you will find rest for your souls. For my yoke is easy and my burden is light. (Matthew 11:29–30)

The emotionally destructive paths that Satan has laid in the lives of many people appear to have no end in sight. He thrives on individuals' miseries. His desire is to cripple you emotionally, spiritually, and physically so that you hate everything about yourself and wonder why you are alive. You are trapped and unable to look back, forward, left, or right. I said this to you: Even under multiple constraints and breakdowns, you have the ability to survive. How? There are three factors:

First, Jesus did all the work for you on that cross. If you have not taken that step to recognize and accept Him, I encourage you to give Him a ring through prayers, and speak to someone at a local church. You are not alone, and you do not deserve to bear those burdens alone. You just have to believe in and accept Jesus in order to be reenergized and to strengthen your ability to look up and forge forward. Satan desires that you stay crippled, emotionally, spiritually, and physically.

Christ, however, desires that you be complete and healthy in every way.

> The thief comes only to steal and kill and destroy; I have come that they may have life, and have it to the full. (John 10:10)

Once you accept and believe in Christ, the traumatic experience becomes crippled in itself and is unable to trap or control you any longer. Do your individual research, pray, and ask questions as much as you want to. There is nothing wrong in doing your research to ensure that what you're being told is correct (Acts 17:11). A leader at a local church would be happy to assist you. The trauma you experienced or the people who did it to you do not have power and control over you. Christ gives you the blessing and opportunity to take your life back from Satan. This can only be accomplished through Christ alone. Why? This is because those burdens are too heavy for you to bear alone. If you believe and trust Christ, lean on Him even more. The one and only safety plan we have is Christ.

Second, remember your personal triumphs. Even though you are limited to how much you can bear emotionally, remember those times in the past when you fought your way out of one trauma, then another. When you get hit with challenging memories of traumatic experiences, remember how strong you were, even though you looked weak at the time. Remember those challenging times you thought you were done and buried—your life was over, hanging on a thread.

If you think deeply about it, you'll see that you can do it again and again with Christ on your side. Sometimes it's difficult to think back on those triumphs because you are fixated on those bad memories. Before you know it, hate, resentment, revenge, discord, and irritation creeps in, overtakes you, and dwells in you—these are fruits of the devil.

> But the fruit of the Spirit is love, joy, peace, forbearance, kindness, goodness, faithfulness, gentleness and self-control. Against such things there is no law. (Galatians 5:22–23)

You do not want or need them. They will keep you miserable. They will lead you in the wrong direction with the wrong people and the wrong places, and you'll be unable to live your life to your full potential.

Third, countless issues hold us captive in many ways—some we observed and others we did not. They affect our actions and words in many areas of our lives. Sometimes, we become slaves to so many things in our lives that we find it difficult to exist as were destined to by God. In the same way, we consciously and unconsciously become captives to our circumstances but also are in bondage to the same people who were responsible for our traumas. Once we are in bondage to those vicious traumatic experiences and to the perpetrators of those experiences, we feeling suffocated. Even though we are disconnected from the perpetrators and think that we will never see or hear from them again, we may continue to maintain the same vicious cycles by engaging in unhealthy or abusive relationships because that's all we know. We may become numb to what's happening and feel as if it is normal for others to treat us that way. Such situations bring even more chaos into our lives, and we never grow out of it. Initially, we thought we made the right decision to disconnect from them, but we may unconsciously run toward them, as if we haven't had enough trauma. The trend continues from one abusive relationship to another.

Remember, just because you shut someone out of your life and threw away the keys doesn't mean it's over. Your good, bad, and ugly experiences become part of who you are. So, what is the solution to being freed from the bondage of people who traumatized you? Forgiveness is the solution. I understand how difficult it is to forgive the people who did those things own your mind while you are awake and while you are asleep. How do I know this? Just examine your triggers. I encourage you to seek mental health services in order to properly examine your triggers. Seek Christian counselors to guide and help you navigate through your bondage. Review chapter 2 of this book to gain more insight on how to proceed.

Healing through Forgiveness

Song: "Healing Rain" by Michael W. Smith

What do we gain from forgiving someone? Due to our human limitations, forgiveness can be unrealistic.

> When your heart has been shattered and reshaped into something that doesn't quite feel normal inside your own chest yet, forgiveness is a bit unrealistic. (TerKeurst 2020, 17)

This means that due to our human nature, it is impossible for us to totally forgive. Forgiveness isn't easy because any type of hurt is real; due to human nature, it is hard to let go. I tell you this with full confidence, however, that with Christ in your life, it will be easy. Seek His face with a contrite heart. Trust and believe in Him. Then, the healing rain will pour into your mind, body, and spirit. Christ is the beginning of your healing process. I also want to make it clear that forgiveness doesn't mean you have to go back and put yourself in harm's way. Forgiveness can occur without restoring the relationship. It may also depend on what you are forgiving and the degree or severity of the matter.

> Many people have the mistaken idea that if someone has hurt them and they forgive the person, they will have to go back and suffer through the same hurt all over again. They think that in order to forgive, they must enter back into an active relationship with the person who has injured them. That is not true, and the misconception has caused a problem for many people who want to forgive. Forgiveness does not necessarily mean restoration. (Meyer 2008, 63)

Your healing cannot begin until you forgive. Forgiveness and healing are siblings and each cannot do without the other. This is difficult, but through God, this is possible. You need to heal in order to bloom. What happened to you was not fair, however many times it happened. The physical or emotional scars will never go away, but those scars do not have an ounce of control over you. Not forgiving will continue to control every step you make, everywhere you turn, and everything you touch.

Some people have shared that they go to bed in tears and wake up in the morning in tears. I realized this was a routine for them, and the strategies they implemented every day, from the time they woke up until they went to bed, were used to cope.

Remember that you have survived to this day, and Christ wants you to hand over to Him those burdens you are carrying. Again, this will not be easy, but take a minute to remember how much Christ's body was battered. If you cannot trust anyone, trust Christ, and you will not be disappointed. All individuals need to move on with their lives and to enjoy the persons they are. Unforgiven matters will continue to hold you down if you do not take that step. It is not an easy step, but it is highly necessary because you deserve to move on to better things.

When past wrongs done to you are not forgiven, triggers of those traumas will continue to impact you in negative ways. Your reactions to certain discussions, music, voices, noise, television programs, sounds, and so forth will trigger you to react negatively. Each negative impact you experience will continue to psychologically delay you. In some cases, people make progress for a whole day but crash the next day because of triggers. Then, the loss ignites anger, frustration, irritation, restlessness, depression, or anxiety. All of a sudden, your mood goes sour, and you find yourself in a defensive or annoyed mood with people around you. Such an emotional state can lead you to lash out or speak unwisely to others.

> Unhealed hurt often becomes unleashed hurt spewed out on others. (TerKeurst 2020, 23)

Sometimes, you may realize that you handled the situation wrong, and sometimes you may not even recall what happened because you experienced an emotional blackout. There goes your day that began well. You continue to remain within the fragile zone with one step forward and one step backward. Unfortunately, the record playing in your mind of those incidents—what was said, done, or felt—may not go away. It becomes part of who you are, but they should not deprive, prevent, or cripple you. This is why forgiveness is crucial, as then you are less likely to be dominated by negative thoughts or react negatively to triggers.

We pursue total independence from our dark emotional experiences in order to be healed. The one key we view as impossible or unrealistic is the key that opens that door of freedom. The key is forgiveness. I wish I could tell you there is an easier route, but there isn't.

When I arrived in the United States in 1991, I brought with me a lot of baggage of past hurts, some of which I'd suppressed for many years. Most of this hurt was from things my father said to me. Yes, I was brought up in a loving home, but my relationship with my father was extremely strained. Then, I felt as if I was handicapped by the way he treated me. Because I was angry at home and seeking revenge, I would steal his money and give it to others who needed it. I felt that was where I could hit him the hardest. I became obsessed and felt that he had to pay somehow. There was much emotional aggression and abuse when I was home.

From the time I arrived in the States and had extra money, I would send the lion's share to my mother, separately, but very little to my father. He noticed what I was doing and sent me a letter to let me know that he knew what I had been doing. After I got married in 2000, my then-wife stopped me from using that approach, and we sent money to my parents together and equally. I struggled with the idea of dealing with everyone equally and still harbored anger and resentment against him because of one statement he made that I overheard. He did not know I was present, and he was under the influence when he said it, so he might not have remembered saying it. But the statement that sealed the deal for me and confirmed the label I already had given myself was his saying I was handicapped. It was clear to me why he had said the things he said and did the things he did to me. I believed that I was useless, while at the same time, I vowed that I would be better than him in life. A statement such as "You will amount to nothing and be useless throughout your life" has stuck in my head to this day. My self-esteem was in the gutter, and I saw myself as unlovable and incapable. So, how did I get over the hurdle of all the attacks on me?

In 2002, I started pursuing my master's degree at Liberty University. To get into the field of mental health services, it's often encouraged for students to seek counseling to resolve past issues before they are in the position to help others. In my first class, we were asked to think of a person with whom we had conflict (small or large) or who had offended us, and we would forgive by whatever means. The first person who came to mind, of course, was my father. As difficult as it was to do it, I bought a card and sent it to him. In the card, I wrote, "Just wanted to say I love you, and I forgive you."

My mother let me know that he'd received the card, but I did not get a response from him, and he passed away in 2010. I felt a lot better after sending that card and before his death. A massive burden was removed from my shoulders, and I felt lively again. It was not easy, as I was extremely stubborn during that period. It was a process for me that I took one step at a time. Later, I realized that I had not forgiven him, but I did it for myself. I did not wait for his response because I knew it was not necessary. I did my part, and that's what counted.

Everyone is different in how they deal with trauma or the methodologies they apply to help them survive. In chapter 2 of this book, I demonstrated how counseling services can help you work through the traumas you experienced. Counseling services will help you reach the point of forgiveness. In some situations, you may not need to see someone at all, but choosing to make that one life-changing decision will lead you to say, "I forgive." Those words are the most powerful ever, except accepting Christ as your Lord and Savior. Those two words—I forgive—can shatter emotional chains of bondage in pieces through the name of Jesus Christ.

That said, finding the appropriate candidate to help you start making this journey is crucial. Forgiveness is not something that can be done through our human nature. We have limits to how much we can bear. Forgiveness is a spiritual matter that cannot be taken lightly. It can be attained and implemented only through spiritual means (Christ).

Look for a Christian counselor, clergy, lay people from your church, or church members who can assist you through this process. It is not a process you should go through alone. Spiritual support through prayers and fellowship is recommended. You will need as much healthy support as possible. Take whatever time you need before arriving at that point of forgiveness. I will say this—the longer you take, the longer your self-image will continue to suffer. Many have resorted to self-harm and many other dark options (drug abuse, alcohol abuse, etc.) because they hated who they were. The only thing left that they knew was to evolve within the perimeter of their pain, which also left room for despair. Unfortunately, many people have taken their lives because the pain and suffering were too much to bear. We have a "being" waiting for us, to help us remove the pain, to lighten the tons of pain we bear inside, to remove the pain entirely. There is no other way but through Christ. He is our one and only first step to gaining our independence from the chains of pain or past hurt. Without total redemption from Him, the road to forgiveness will be very hazardous. The safest way to go is through Him.

After taking Christ's redemption path, do you have to forgive the person face-to-face or by phone, text, or email? The person does not need to know that you've forgiven him or her. Forgiveness is not for the health of the perpetrator. It is for you and your physical, spiritual, and mental health. It's your decision whether you want the person to know you have forgiven. In my professional experience, a few forgivers expect a response from the perpetrator and get even more hurt when they don't get one. You do not want to set up yourself for failure. Many have contacted the persons who hurt them and never have received an apology or admission they were wrong. I would encourage you not to go that route, and stick with forgiving the person in order to gain back your independence.

In some cases, some people do not like to say, "I am sorry." Maybe it's because of their ego or upbringing. Some may recognize that what they did was not nice and will try to make amends. If they apologize, accept it, just as

Christ has forgiven you. It is too much of a burden to carry this weight on your shoulders. It is not worth it, but I am confident that *you* are worth it. Forgiveness does not mean accepting whatever you can get. Not at all. It's all about you and making yourself feel whole again. You do not need an apology or response or gifts to forgive. Forgiveness is pure and should be viewed in that manner. Why? Because Christ is the author and the model of forgiveness.

> The power of forgiveness is the power of God to transform us from inside out. Jesus is our example and role model for every aspect of our lives, and He demonstrated how we should live in relationship with other people. (Meyer 2008, 874)

How about forgetting after you forgave? Is that possible? Some people have claimed they were able to forget, but I am not sure if that is true or realistic. Maybe the issues were suppressed. Suppressing emotional hurts can be very risky and dangerous. Let me give you an idea of why that is not advisable. I had a huge meltdown between August and September 2022. One event triggered an avalanche of sadness, and I felt like I was losing my mind. I became overwhelmed. On August 20, I spent some time with close friends at a restaurant. Some of them could tell something was not right with me. Toward the end of our meal, I asked them to pray, as I was preparing to make a decision.

On my way home, I became even more emotional and became teary. That evening, I was overwhelmed by sadness. I processed it and felt like I came to terms with what triggered it. As I was driving home, I prayed and asked God for help. I laid out what I would like to happen. I even said to God, "I'm not asking too much." There was no response for my requests, but I knew He heard my prayers. Then, while at it, my spirit suggested that I text my brother in Christ to check up on him and let him know I was thinking of him and praying for him. At first, I was a bit annoyed that I had asked God some things, and He redirected my mind to pray for someone else. I could not comprehend it. When I got home, however, and closed the garage, I texted him to let him know I was thinking of him and praying for him.

His response? His text was timely and shared some information with me. I felt like the Spirit had let me know that it wasn't about me that evening but someone else. Did it mean God ignored my prayers? No, not at all. Praying, however, is not always about me, which I learned that evening. I continued to feel like I was in mourning, though, and could not tell why.

When my coworker Kara came to work one Monday, I was still broken down and could not pinpoint what was going on. I said that I felt like I was mourning something but was not sure what it was. She was confused as well. This went on from August through the middle of September 2022. Then, I decided to dig deeper and found out that my mother had passed away in September 2005. The foster child we thought we would adopt went back home to his parents in September 2005, and he turned nineteen in the same month. And my best friend passed away in September. Reasons behind my mourning came to the surface as I was crumbling emotionally. I did suppress a lot, unconsciously, and most of the events happened in September, as you can see. It was awful.

Then I got back from my trip, and my neighbors, Pete and Sherry, informed me that their dog, Izzy (a poodle) had passed away the same day I'd left Florida for Helen, Georgia. This is why it's a great idea to bring as much as you can to the surface so you can deal with it effectively. That said, you will need an expert to guide you through the process; don't try to self-diagnosis, as that is very dangerous. A lot of information is available on the internet nowadays, but I suggest that you avoid those traps. Whatever it is you are going through, you deserve to heal properly and with confidence and through the grace of God. Many mental health counselors are standing by to help.

Not everyone has insurance coverage to address their mental health needs, but nonprofit counseling organizations may offer a sliding scale. Don't let ego or stubbornness get in the way. Your mental health needs should not be ignored. They are silent crises waiting to explode, and you have no idea when, how, or where it will happen. Seek help as soon as you can.

No one or nothing can control our existence, except God. Let's not allow the fruits of the devil to overtake our hearts.

> Trusting God completely means having faith that He knows what is best for your life. You expect him to keep His promises, help you with problems, and do the impossible when necessary. (Warren 2002)

He modeled forgiveness. He made forgiveness possible. And He tells and shows us that forgiveness is necessary. You do not have to put yourself in harm's way to forgive. You can do so wherever you are and regardless of what you are doing. You can do it regardless if the person knows or not. Trust God, and you will never be disappointed.

In closing, I will say this: If I have hurt you, I am sorry and hope you can forgive me. If you have done anything wrong to me, I forgive you. Christ loves you, and so do I.

Song: "Forgiveness" by Matthew West

The Lord bless you and keep you; the Lord make his face shine on you and be gracious to you; the Lord turn his face toward you and give you peace.
—Numbers 6:24–26

Song: "The Blessing" by Kari Jobe and Cody Carnes

REFERENCES

American Psychiatric Association. 2013. *Diagnostic and Statistical Manual of Mental Disorders*, Fifth Edition. Washington, DC: American Psychiatric Publishing.

Angelica, E. 2001. *The Fieldstone Alliance Nonprofit Guide to Crafting Effective Mission and Vision Statements.* Saint Paul, MN: Fieldstone Alliance.

Anyiam, E. 2022. *Embracing Life: Surviving the Struggle by Learning to Embrace the Experience.* Bloomington, IN: WestBow Press.

Barrett, T., and J. Barrett. 2018. *Ultimate Aptitude Tests: Over 1000 Practice Questions for Abstract Visual, Numerical, Verbal, Physical, Spatial and Systems Tests.* NY: Kogan Page.

Beck, J. R. 1999. *Jesus & Personality Theory: Exploring the Five-Factor Model.* Downers Grove, IL: InterVarsity Press.

Chapman, G. 1992. *The Five Love Languages: How to Express Heartfelt Commitment to Your Mate.* Chicago: Northfield.

Cherry, K. Updated July 28, 2022. "How the Myers-Briggs Type Indicator Works." VeryWellMind. https://www.verywellmind.com/the-myers-briggs-indicator-2795583.

Clay, D. 2018. *How to Write the Perfect Resume: Stand Out, Land Interviews, and Get the Job You Want.* Danclay.com/perfectresume.

Cohen, A. H. 2002. *Why Your Life Sucks: and What You Can Do about It.* NY, NY: Bantam Dell.

Collins, G. R. 1993. *The Biblical Basis of Christian Counseling for People Helpers.* Colorado Springs, CO: NavPress.

Deere, J. 2018. *Even in Our Darkness: A Story of Beauty in a Broken Life.* Grand Rapids, MI: Zondervan.

Drenth, Dr. A. J. 2017. *My True Type: Clarifying Your Personality Type, Preference and Functions.* Columbia, SC: Andrew Drenth.

Drenth, Dr. A. J. 2017. *The 16 Personality Types: Profiles, Theory and Type Development.* Orlando, FL: Inquire Books.

Eagleman, D. 2015. *The Brain: The Story of You.* NY: Pantheon Books.

Evans, A. 1995. *Returning to Your First Love.* Chicago, IL: Moody Press.

Frank, B. 2022. *The Science of Stuck: Breaking through Inertia to Find Your Path Forward.* New York, NY: TarcherPerigee.

Frank, R. April 1, 2022. "Soaring markets helped the richest 1% gain $6.5 trillion in wealth last year, according to the Fed." CNBC. https://www.cnbc.com/2022/04/01/richest-one-percent-gained-trillions-in-wealth-2021.html.

Frankl, V. E. 2006. *Man's Search for Meaning.* Boston, MA: Beacon Press.

Gauthier, P. 2022. *One Baptism: The Power of Water and the Spirit.* Bloomington, IN: WestBow Press.

Glen, J. 2020. *Wealth Inequality in America: Causes, Consequences and Solutions: The Destruction of the Middle Class*. Orlando, FL: Pensiero Press.

Graham, B. 1978. *The Holy Spirit: Activating God's Power in Your Life*. Nashville, TN: Thomas Nelson.

Grudem, W. 1994. *Systematic Theology: An Introduction to Biblical Doctrine*. Grand Rapids, MI: Zondervan.

Hart, L. A. 1975. *How The Brain Works: A New Understanding of Human Learning, Emotion, and Thinking*. NY: Basic Books. Inc.

Ingram, L. November 2, 2022. "Minnesota Woman Gunned Down Outside Her Office After Rejecting Co-worker's Advances." Fox News. https://www.foxnews.com/us/minnesota-woman-gunned-down-outside-office-rejecting-co-workers-advances.

Jeremiah, Dr. D. 2016. *Is This the End?: Signs of God's Providence in a Disturbing New World*. Nashville, TN: W Publishing Group.

Jeremiah, Dr. D. 1997. *Christ's Death & Resurrection*. Atlanta, GA: Walk Through the Bible Ministries.

Jeremiah, Dr. D. 2020. *Forward: Discovering God's Presence and Purpose in Your Tomorrow*. Nashville, TN: W. Publishing.

Kendrick, M. 2015. *Your Blueprint for Life: How to Align Your Passion, Gifts and Calling with Eternity in Mind*. Nashville, TN: Thomas Nelson.

Kise, J. G., D. Stark, and S. K. Hirsh. 2005. *LifeKeys: Discover Who You Are*. Minneapolis, MN: Bethany House Publishers.

Koltuska-Haskin, B. 2020. *How My Brain Works: A Guide to Understanding It Better and Keeping It Healthy*. Santa Fe, NM: Golden Word Books.

Leaf, C. 2021. *Cleaning Up Your Mental Mess: 5 Simple, Scientifically Proven Steps to Reduce Anxiety, Stress and Toxic Thinking*. Grand Rapids, MI: Baker Books.

Lane, T. S., and P. D. Tripp. 2008. *Relationships: A Mess Worth Making*. Greensboro, NC: New Growth Press.

Livingston, L. W. 2020. *A Life Living Fate*. Bloomington, IN: Xlibris.

Livingston, G. 2009. *How to Love: Choosing Well at Every Stage of Life*. Cambridge, MA: Da Capo Press.

Lucado, M. 2017. *Anxious for Nothing: Finding the Calm in a Chaotic World*. Nashville, TN: Thomas Nelson.

Lucado, M. 2020. *Facing Your Giants: God Still Does the Impossible*. Nashville, TN: Thomas Nelson.
Lucado, M. 2020. *God Will Help You*. Nashville, TN: Thomas Nelson.
Lucado, M. 2018. *Life Lessons from Galatians: Free in Christ*. Nashville, TN: Thomas Nelson.
Lucado, M. 1986. *No Wonder They Call Him the Savior*. Colorado Springs, CO: Multnomah Press.

Lucado, M. 1989. *Six Hours One Friday: Anchoring to the Power of the Cross*. Colorado Springs, CO: Multnomah Books.

Lucado, M. 2021. *You Were Made for This Moment: Courage for Today and Hope for Tomorrow*. Nashville, TN: Thomas Nelson.

Lucas, J. 2001. *Learning How to Learn: The Ultimate Learning and Memory Instruction.* Dallas, TX: Lucas Education.

McLemore, C W. 1974. *Clergyman's Psychological Handbook: Clinical Information for Pastoral Counseling.* Grand Rapids, MI.

McDowell, J., and S. McDowell. 2015. *More than a Carpenter.* Coral Stream, IL: Tyndale House Publishers.

Mitchell, D. 2019. *The Power of Understanding Yourself: The Key to Self-Discovery, Personal Development, and Being the Best You.* Hoboken, NJ: Wiley.

Merriam-Webster's Dictionary of Law. 2011. Springfield, MA: Merriam-Webster, Inc.

Meyer, J. 2008. *The Power of Forgiveness: Keep Your Heart Free.* Minneapolis, MN: Koechel Peterson & Associates, Inc.

Mother Teresa and T. Moore. 2010. *No Greater Love.* Novato, CA: New World Library.

Mora, Dr. F. 2022. *Free will Choice: The Story.* Bloomington, IN: WestBow Press.

Murray, A. 2011. *The True Vine: Meditation for a Month on John 15:1–16.* Chicago, IL: Moody Publishers,

Nichols, M. P. 2016. *Family Therapy Concepts and Methods.* Boston, MA: Pearson.

Oxford Languages. 2008. *Little Oxford Dictionary and Thesaurus.* Oxford: University Press.

Page, S. B. 2006. *Establishing a System of Policies and Procedures: Basics of developing a policies and procedures program and using a writing format for policies and procedures.* www.companymanuels.com/index.htm.

Packer, J. I. 1995. *Daily Devotions: Knowing and Doing the Will of God.* Ann Arbor, MI: Servant Publications.

Perry, T. 2017. *Higher Is Waiting.* NY: Spiegel & Grau.

Ratey, J. J. 2018. *The User's Guide to the Brain: Perception, Attention, and the Four Theaters of the Brain.* NY: Pantheon Books.

Respectfully Quoted: A Dictionary of Quotations. 2010. Compiled by the Library of Congress. Washington, DC: Congressional Quarterly Inc.

Rosenberg, R. November 2, 2022. "Minnesota Woman Gunned Down Outside Her Office after Rejecting Coworker's Advances." Fox News. https://www.foxnews.com/us/minnesota-woman-gunned-down-outside-office-rejecting-co-workers-advances.

Russell, K., and P. Carter. 2015. *Ultimate IQ Tests: 1000 Practice Questions to Boost Your Brainpower.* NY: Kogan Page.

Rycroft, R. S., and K. L. Kinsley. 2021. *Inequality in America: Causes and Consequences.* Denver, CO: ABC-CLIO.

Selenee, M. 2021. *Connected Fates, Separate Destinies: Using Family Constellations Therapy to Recover from Inherited Stories and Trauma.* Hay House, Inc.

Sessions, M. 2019. *The Handbook to You: Discover How You Are Programmed and How to Live Your Life to the Fullest.* Jones Media Publishing.

Sherman, D., and W. Hendricks. 1987. *Your Work Matters to God*. Colorado Springs, Colorado: NavPress.

Short, L. 2014. *Finding Faith in the Dark: When the Story of Your Life Takes a Turn You Didn't Plan*. Grand Rapids, MI: Zondervan

Simpson, A. B. 2014. *Walking in the Spirit*. CreateSpace Independent Publishing Platform.

Stanley, C. 2010. *Ministering through Spiritual Gifts: Recognize Your Personal Gifts and Use Them to Further the Kingdom*. Nashville, TN: Thomas Nelson, Inc.

Stott, J. 2021. *Baptism and Fullness: The Work of the Holy Spirit Today*. Leicester, England: Inter-Varsity Press.

Stone, W. C. 2016. *Believe and Achieve: 17 Principles of Success*. Shippensburg, PA: Sound Wisdom.

Sterling Education. 2022. *Civil Procedure: Essential Law Self-Teaching Guide:* Boston, MA.

Tanzi, A., and M. Dorning. October 8, 2021. "Top 1% of U.S. Earners Now Hold More Wealth Than All of the Middle Class." Bloomberg. https://www.bloomberg.com/news/articles/2021-10-08/top-1-earners-hold-more-wealth-than-the-u-s-middle-class#xj4y7vzkg.

TerKeurst, L. 2020. *Forgiving What You Can't Forget: Discover How to Move On, Make Peace with Painful Memories, and Create a Life That's Beautiful Again*. Nashville, TN: Nelson Books.

Thompson, J. October 13, 2022. "How to Protect Yourself from Romance Scams." Newsweek. https://www.newsweek.com/man-claiming-russian-astronaut-iss-fraud-japan-woman-1751475

Thompson, L. 1998. *Personality Type: An Owner's Manual: A Practice Guide to Understanding Yourself and Others through Typology*. Boston, MA: Shambhala Publications.

Tozer, A. W. 2020. *No Greater Love: Experiencing the Heart of Jesus*. Minneapolis, MN: Bethany House.

Tozer. A. W. 2016. *Prayer: Communing with God in Everything—Collected Insights*. Chicago, IL: Moody Publishers.

Tozer, A.W. 1976. *Who Put Jesus on the Cross?: And Other Questions of the Christian Faith*. WingSpread.

United States Census Bureau. 2022. Population Clock. https://www.census.gov/popclock.

Warren, R. 2002. *The Purpose Driven Life: What on Earth Am I Here for?* Grand Rapids, MI: Zondervan.

Wiersbe, W. W. 1979. *The Strategy of Satan: How to Detect & Defeat Him*. Carol Stream, IL: Tyndale House Publishers, Inc.

Printed in the United States
by Baker & Taylor Publisher Services